❰ ❰ ❰   THE INDIANS OF IOWA

 A BUR OAK BOOK

THE INDIANS OF IOWA

By Lance M. Foster

University of Iowa Press, Iowa City

University of Iowa Press, Iowa City 52242
Copyright © 2009 by the University of Iowa Press
www.uiowapress.org
Printed in the United States of America

Design by Ashley Muehlbauer

The University of Iowa Press is a member of Green
Press Initiative and is committed to preserving
natural resources.

Printed on acid-free paper

Library of Congress Cataloging-in-Publication Data
Foster, Lance M., 1960–
   The Indians of Iowa / by Lance M. Foster.
      p.   cm.
"A Bur Oak Book."
Includes bibliographical references and index.
ISBN-13: 978-1-58729-817-2 (pbk.)
ISBN-10: 1-58729-817-1 (pbk.)
1. Indians of North America—Iowa—History.
2. Iowa—Antiquities. I. Title.
E78.I6F67 2009   2009006877
977.7'01—dc22

The board of directors of the State Historical Society
of Iowa, Inc., made a generous contribution toward
the publication of this book.

For my family

That hand is not the color of yours. But if I pierce it, I shall feel pain. The blood that will flow from mine will be of the same color as yours. I am a man. The same God made us both.

CHIEF STANDING BEAR, Ponca, 1879

CONTENTS

ACKNOWLEDGMENTS

I wish to give special thanks to the following people and organizations that have helped or inspired me in various ways over the years. Some have moved on, but I acknowledge them here in the context in which I knew them.

First is my family, my clan, and my Ioway people, those still with us and those who have gone, with a special mention of my parents, Gary and Rita, and my grandparents, George N. and Esteline and George W. and Ava, and all my many elders and relatives as well as my siblings Garth, Bryan, Brandi, and Amber and their families and all my Ioway *wodi*, especially the Pete Fee family and the Robert and Glenda Fields family. It would take another book to name all my elders, relations, and friends from our Ioway people.

I would also like to thank the Meskwaki people I came to know during my time in Iowa, notably the Homer Bear family, Johnathan Buffalo, Don Wanatee, and Ray Young Bear. Other tribal people I must thank are those in Iowa who gave me their friendship and knowledge, including the Jerry Stubben family (Ponca), the Smokey McKinney family (Potawatomi), the Maria Pearson family (Yankton Sioux), Irma Wilson White (Winnebago-Omaha), and Lynn Paxson (Cherokee).

I also acknowledge those friends in Montana who gave me and my family their friendship and knowledge, including among the northern Cheyenne the families of Herman Bear Comes Out, John Woodenlegs, and Austin Two Moons as well as Leroy "Eddie" Barbeau of Helena (Ojibwa). I also want to remember those folks I knew at the University of Montana, notably in the Native American Studies Department and Kyi-Yo Indian Club, and at the Institute of American Indian Arts in Santa Fe.

I want to acknowledge and thank the various people I came to know during my time at Iowa State University, especially my major professor in anthropology and mentor David Gradwohl and his wife, Hanna, and my major professor in landscape architecture Robert Harvey and his wife, Ann, as well as George Jackson, Tim and Genevieve Keller, Nancy Osborn, Steve Pett, John Weinkein, Mike and Mary Warren, and Norma Wolff. I want to acknowledge from Iowa's Office of the State Archaeologist Lynn Alex, William Green, and K. Kris Hirst; from the State Historical Society of Iowa Jerome Thompson, Kathy Gourley, and Doug Jones; and from Luther College Lori Stanley. I also wish to thank Mildred Mott Wedel, scholar of the Ioway par excellence, and my editor Holly Carver and her excellent staff at the University of Iowa Press, whose patience and persistence finally brought this project to fruition. There are so many over the years who have helped in their own ways. I apologize for those I have left out, but you know who you are, and I think of you and wish you well.

Finally, I wish to thank my wife, Lisa, for her love, knowledge, and unfailing support for years through even the darkest of hours. I couldn't have done this without her.

PREFACE

The story of the Indians of Iowa is a long and complex one. The purpose of this book is to provide an introduction to this story.

As a member of the Ioway tribe, an archaeologist, and a scholar of Native American studies, I chose to go to Iowa State University for my graduate studies in 1991. For the following six years, from 1991 to 1997, I lived in Ames, traveling throughout Iowa, meeting people, and learning about the past of my tribe and about the other nations that shared the Land between Two Rivers.

When I first began to explore the Internet in 1994, I was eager to see what might be online about the Ioway and the other tribes of Iowa. When I did a search using the terms "Indian" and "Iowa," the only site I could find was the Fluxus Indian Museum, which was really about an art movement rather than the historical tribes of Iowa. I decided to put together a series of articles about the tribes of Iowa on my ISU student homepage, Native Nations of Iowa, with the first version going online early in 1996. As a member of the Ioway tribe, I thought it was important to introduce the public to the story of the native peoples of this state. After I put up the site, I received an e-mail message from an anthropology professor at the University of Iowa, thanking me for the information and revealing that scholars had been teaching for over twenty years that the Ioway tribe was extinct. Obviously there was a need for good information, and it was very exciting to be part of the Internet revolution.

Many different Indian tribes have lived in Iowa throughout time. Each of them existed as an independent nation, with its own history, culture, language, and traditions. Some, such as the Ioway and Otoe, were residents from before recorded time until after the coming of white settlers. Other tribes, like the Omaha and Ponca, moved to new territories long before white settlers arrived or used Iowa mostly for hunting grounds, like the Pawnee. We know about these earliest residents through tribal oral tradition and archaeological evidence.

Other nations, like the Sioux, Sauk, and Meskwaki, are so much part of Iowa's history from the earliest written accounts by European explorers that they may be considered native to Iowa. Still others, like the Potawatomi, Winnebago, and Illinois, lived in Iowa for a relatively short time but played memorable roles in Iowa's history. Finally, many other tribes, such as the Huron, Mascouten, Ojibwa, and Miami, visited Iowa briefly during hunting trips or times of war, for plunder or refuge. Today, only the Meskwaki have a community settlement in Iowa, although the Omaha and Winnebago own small parcels of land as well.

In this book you will learn about all these Indian nations with emphasis on the tribes most connected to Iowa history and archaeology. This book will use the terms "Indian" and "Native American" interchangeably, though most prefer to be called by their individual tribal name, such as Meskwaki or Omaha, and secondarily as Indian.

Tribes are listed alphabetically, though some are grouped together that, while distinct politically, are closely related to each other in culture and in Iowa history. In between the tribal entries, sections called "A Closer Look" focus on topics such as archaeology, traditional lifestyles, arts, genealogy, and native languages. At the end of the book are sections on places to visit as well as resources for those seeking more information.

Most people have never heard of the richness of the native legacy here in Iowa. Many across America have associated the story of the American Indian only with states like Arizona or Oklahoma. But every single state, every square mile of our country, has its own rich and complex story of its own native nations and the lands which sustained them from time immemorial. Iowa is no exception. I hope that you will be inspired to learn more about the place that you call home and the people who long ago also called it home.

❨ ❨ ❨   THE INDIANS OF IOWA

LEWIS AND CLARK IN NATIVE IOWA

❰ ❰ ❰

The years 2004 to 2006 marked the bicentennial of Lewis and Clark's journey up the Missouri River. One of their main tasks was to contact Indian tribes along the route. Though they did meet several of the native nations associated with Iowa, they did not meet any Indians who were then living in Iowa. For over a month on their upstream voyage in 1804, Lewis and Clark traveled along the looping meanders of the Missouri River adjacent to western Iowa, until they passed the mouth of the Big Sioux River.

Lewis and Clark's party camped for several days in July in hopes of contacting the Pawnee, the Omaha, and the Otoe. The Otoe, who had recently been joined by the Missouria, had their village in Nebraska, a few miles up the Platte River, near the Pawnee. The Otoe-Missouria and the Omaha had recently been pushed westward from Iowa by the Yankton Sioux, though they still often hunted in the Loess Hills of Iowa. Lewis and Clark sent men to the villages, but they found them deserted, as the tribes were farther west on the open plains, hunting buffalo.

The explorers finally succeeded in contacting the Otoe-Missouria but not the Omaha or Pawnee. Their initial meeting was with a Missouria man who said the main leaders were out with most of the tribe on the hunt. Lewis and Clark made arrangements for a meeting with some of the minor Otoe-Missouria chiefs and set up camp on the Nebraska side, calling this campsite Handsome Prairie or Council Bluffs. It was located near present-day Blair, Nebraska; Fort Atkinson would be built there a few years later on their recommendation. Council Bluffs, across the Missouri River in Iowa, was named in commemoration of this first council between Lewis and Clark and the Indians of the Missouri. The meeting of August 3, 1804, went well, and the two groups exchanged gifts.

Farther upriver, Lewis and Clark tried to contact the Omaha, but that tribe too was away hunting buffalo. However, they did succeed then in locating the principal chiefs of the Otoe, who wished their assistance in making peace with the elusive Omaha. On August 18, the Otoe met with Lewis and Clark at a campsite near the abandoned Omaha village. The Indians had captured Moses Reed, one of two deserters from the explorers' party, and pled for lenience for him. Though Lewis and Clark could have sentenced him to death, they instead made Reed run a gauntlet made up of the explorers' party. The next day Lewis and Clark held another Otoe council, this time with the real authority for the tribe. The Otoe were dressed in breech-cloths and painted buffalo robes, and some trade blankets were also noted. Presents were exchanged and speeches given; soon Lewis and Clark were again headed upriver. They would next meet the Yankton Sioux, in what would someday become South Dakota.

On their return trip down the Missouri in 1806, Lewis and Clark traveled very quickly, with the river current at times helping them make over sixty miles a day. During this trip they did not meet any Indians along the Iowa stretch, but almost every day they met at least one party of traders going upstream to trade with tribes like the Omaha and Pawnee—a sign of the great changes to come.

What about the other tribes listed in this book as being among the native nations of Iowa? Though other tribes did hunt along the Missouri, many of them still concentrated their activities along the Mississippi and its tributaries. Lewis and Clark mentioned seeing an abandoned Ioway village in 1804, located on the Missouri River near what is now Council Bluffs, Iowa. Between 1804 and 1806, most of the Ioway were located in the interior of Iowa, with the major village at Iowaville on the lower Des Moines River. The Sioux controlled the upper Des Moines basin and most of northern Iowa, with the Yankton in the west and the Santee (primarily Wahpekute) in the east. The Sauk still had their major village at Rock Island, and it would be almost thirty years before the Black Hawk War. The Meskwaki were mining lead at Dubuque and living throughout eastern Iowa. The remnants of the Illinois Confederacy had just finished agreement with the 1803 Treaty of Vincennes, and they were moving from their last bits of land in Illinois into Missouri. Some tribes had not yet entered Iowa. The Winnebago were still in their Wisconsin homelands. The Potawatomi were in Indiana and Illinois, though treaties were badly eroding their land base.

The Indian nations undoubtedly believed Lewis and Clark's small party to be just another transient group of white traders passing through on their way to establish trade, as had many before them. After all, the French had been trading goods on the upper Mississippi and across to the Missouri for over a hundred years. And the British and Spanish had also been trading for several decades. Of what significance could yet another party of white explorers be?

But Lewis and Clark were the vanguard for the American people who would sweep westward into Iowa, not just to trade but to settle and farm the land. In fact, while Lewis and Clark were traveling upriver, down in St. Louis the first of several treaties ceding land to the United States would begin the inevitable flood of white settlers. How could the Indians ever conceive that a party of a few dozen men represented the end of their way of life and the loss of all their lands? By the time one of the young Otoe boys or girls who saw Lewis and Clark in 1804 had reached the age of sixty, it was all over. Native Iowa was no more.

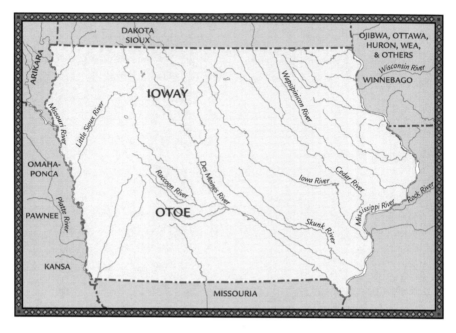

General locations of Indian tribes in and near Iowa, ca. 1720s. Ioway and Otoe dominate all of Iowa, sharing territory with the Omaha and Ponca and other tribes in the western fringe and with the Huron, Ottawa, Winnebago, and others in the northeast. Information about tribes in this early period is notoriously unreliable, based as it is on the accounts of Euro-American explorers who had no context in which to understand the peoples and languages they encountered.

Facing page, top map: General locations of tribes, forts, and settlers in 1840s Iowa. Numerous tribes were either established in southwest Iowa near the mouth of the Platte River, sometimes for brief periods, or retained hunting rights there. Adapted from "Cementing American Control, 1816 to 1853: The Historical Context" by Kathryn E. M. Gourley in Whittaker 2009.

Facing page, bottom map: Historic Indian land cessions in Iowa. Iowa tribes had signed more than thirty treaties by 1853, when the last of the Sioux officially were removed from the state. Although a single treaty is often associated with only one tribe, it often affected more than one tribe. Adapted from "Dispossession of the Tribe" by F. A. Auman, *Palimpsest* 38 (1957).

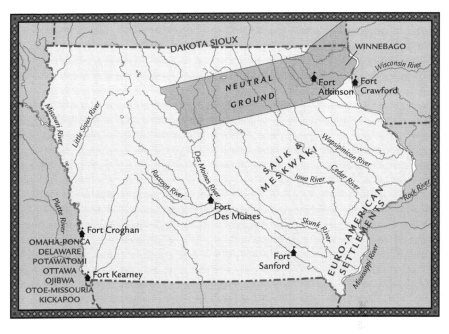

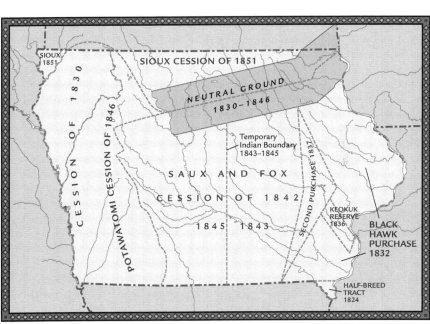

IOWAY

Name means: "Sleepy Ones," derived from Sioux
Other names: Iowa, Baxoje, Bah-Kho-Je
They call themselves: Baxoje, "Gray Heads" or "Gray Snow";
　　Chikiwere, "People of This Place"
Language spoken/language family: Ioway/Chiwere Siouan
Residence in Iowa: Prehistory to 1837
Location today: Iowa Tribe of Kansas and Nebraska near
　　White Cloud, Kansas; Iowa Tribe of Oklahoma near
　　Perkins, Oklahoma

❨ ❨ ❨

The Ioway are best known today as the tribe for whom the state of Iowa was named. They are often called the Ioway to help distinguish them from the state of Iowa. Tribal members use both Iowa and Ioway, although the legal names of both tribes today use "Iowa." The Ioway language belongs to the Siouan family and is closely related to Otoe, Missouria, and Winnebago and more distantly related to Omaha and Dakota. The Ioway and Otoe-Missouria languages are called Chiwere by linguists, after Jiwere, the Otoe name for themselves.

By the time white settlers first entered Iowa in the mid 1800s, the Ioway had moved their villages into northern Missouri, due to pressure and incessant warfare in Iowa between the Sioux in the northern and western parts of the state and the Sauk and Meskwaki in the southern and eastern parts of the state.

Archaeologists call the sites of the ancestral Ioway Oneota, after one of the names for the Upper Iowa River, where such sites were first located. Other closely related tribes such as the Otoe, Missouri, Winnebago, and Omaha also participated in the Oneota culture. This connection is supported by tribal traditions and linguistic studies, which assert that all those tribes were once one people. The Oneota are most identified with certain types of pottery but also with the use of pipestone, copper, and small, triangular arrowheads. They were guardians of the pipestone quarry in Minnesota until about 1700. Many of the sites currently well established as ancestral Ioway sites are in northeast Iowa. Other Ioway villages were located at Blood Run in northwestern Iowa, Iowaville near Selma, and Council Bluffs. The most important villages were located along Iowa's major river systems—the Mississippi, the Upper Iowa River, the Iowa River, the Missouri, the Big Sioux, the Grand River, and the Des Moines River—and around Okoboji Lake and Spirit Lake.

The Ioway were closely related by language and culture to their Sioux kin, but conflict over territory in northern Iowa and southern Minnesota began in the 1600s as a domino effect of the Beaver Wars, conflicts over the fur trade in the east. The Ioway accommodated settlement in eastern Iowa by the Meskwaki by 1730, after that tribe's disastrous wars with the French. Then the Meskwaki-Sauk alliance against the Sioux pulled the Ioway into intense intertribal wars from 1720 to 1845.

During the series of treaties made between 1804 and 1838, in order to defend their claims against those of other tribes like the Sauk, Meskwaki, and Sioux, the Ioway showed maps they had made that located ancestral villages in Iowa. The most famous of these maps was presented by Chief No Heart in connection with the treaty of 1837. Although No Heart's map showed clearly the antiquity of Ioway villages along most of Iowa's major rivers, the United States decided in favor of the claims of the more numerous and powerful Sioux, Sauk, and Meskwaki.

During the early 1800s, the Ioway continued to hunt in the intertribal hunting grounds in western Iowa, along with the Sioux, Omaha, Otoe, Pawnee, and others. Successive treaties made the Ioway and the others surrender title to those western Iowa lands.

In 1836 the Ioway signed a treaty that moved them by 1837 to a new reservation in Kansas and Nebraska. Successive treaties shrank that reservation, and by 1880 part of the tribe began moving to Indian Territory (now Oklahoma). Today there are two groups of Ioway people, the Iowa Tribe of Kansas and Nebraska and the Iowa Tribe of Oklahoma, although members are scattered across the nation. Some still speak a little of the language and attend powwows and other clan functions such as funerals.

Traditional Culture

Ioway society was based on clan membership, passed on to both sons and daughters through the father. Clans included the Bear, the Buffalo, the Wolf, the Thunder-Eagle, the Pigeon, the Elk, the Beaver, and the Snake. Each clan had its own special responsibilities, such as the Thunder clan's leadership in warfare. Each clan also had its own medicine pipe bundle. The Ioway had many religious societies, including the Bear and Buffalo Doctors, who healed wounds, and the Medicine Lodge. The Pipe Dance was the basis for intertribal alliances. Tattooing was also important for young women of special status and for accomplished warriors.

Ioway warfare was centered on warbundles, which provided the war party with spiritual power. Like other tribes, the Ioway had graded war honors for accomplishments like scalping the enemy and counting coup. The Ioway warriors shaved their heads except for their scalplock, to which deer tail roaches were tied.

Ioway houses were of various kinds, including buffalo-hide tipis used during buffalo hunts, oval and square bark lodges used in the summer villages, and smaller mat-covered lodges used during the winter. During the summer, the Ioway grew gardens of corn, beans, and squash near their villages along the major rivers. They went on two annual buffalo hunts on the prairies and hunted deer and small game throughout the year. They also fished and trapped furbearers.

As in other tribes, men were responsible for war and hunting, while women were the homemakers and farmers. Clothing was made of buckskin decorated with quillwork. Men wore little more than loincloths, robes, and moccasins during warm weather. The Ioway quickly adopted European clothing such as the shirt, however, decorating it with trade goods like ribbonwork and beads and mixing it with more traditional buckskin elements.

Famous Ioway

Mahaska I (White Cloud I), his brother No Heart, and Moanahonga (Big Neck or Great Walker) were the most important leaders of the tribe during the treaty period when lands were lost in Iowa. The U.S. government recognized Mahaska I as head chief because of his pro-American stance during the War of 1812. When he was killed, his son, known as Mahaska II and also called Francis "Frank" Whitecloud, and his uncle No Heart finally agreed to remove the Ioway tribe to the new reservation in Kansas. Big Neck refused to go and fought until he was killed. Marie Dorion was an Ioway woman who, like Sacajawea, accompanied explorers up the Missouri River in search of a new passage to the Pacific.

A CLOSER LOOK
Indian Women in Iowa

Most books about Indians focus on the great warriors and chiefs. There are many paintings of famous Indian men but very few of women like Raintchewaime, wife of Mahaska I, a head chief of the Ioway. In early writings women are rarely mentioned and often characterized as little more than drudges who did all the work while the men did all the exciting things.

For Indian people, the reality is more balanced. Men were more visible to outsiders because they engaged in war and defense against other tribes and white intruders. Both women and men, however, had defined tasks needed for tribal survival. With the exception of items like warhorses, clothing, and weapons, women owned everything, including the houses, equipment and tools, and other horses. Women directed most nonwar activities. Women were often the real keepers of the culture, as they were less exposed to the outside world, and they passed traditional teachings on through their children. Women were thus the heart of the tribe; without them, the tribe would cease to exist.

There is some controversy over the term "squaw." Derived from Algonquian tribes back east, this word for "woman" was adopted in English usage to mean any Indian woman. To contemporary Indian women, however, its use can be as charged as the "N-word" is for African Americans. Though it may have had Indian roots, today the word often carries sexist and racist meanings and is offensive.

Several Indian women from Iowa tribes have achieved great fame outside their own communities. Perhaps most historically well known was Ioway Marie Dorion. Like Sacagawea, she guided a party of white explorers to the Pacific. In 1811, five years after Lewis and Clark returned from their historic journey, John Jacob Astor and his Overland Expedition set off to look for a route to the Oregon country, more direct but more difficult than Lewis and Clark's river route. They hired Pierre Dorion as their interpreter, and his wife, Marie, insisted on coming with them. She had two small children and was pregnant with a third. Marie served as interpreter, guide, and peacemaker. After some near disasters, the party made it successfully to the Pacific and founded Astoria, Oregon. On the return trip in 1813, most of the party was massacred, but Marie hid and escaped with her children. Alone, she led them to safety through 250 miles in the dead of winter, surviving on tree bark and boiled hides. She finally found refuge among the Umatilla tribe. Marie never returned to the Midwest but remarried and raised her family in Oregon. She is counted as the first woman to set foot on what would become the Oregon Trail, and a park in Oregon bears her name.

There are many other native women of Iowa whose stories need to be told. Maria Pearson, also known as Running Moccasin, a Yankton Sioux activist, was most famous for her work with the archaeological community. Her efforts led to the protection of burials in Iowa, regardless of race, and ultimately helped lead to a national law, the Native American Graves Protection and Repatriation Act.

In 1993 Adeline Wanatee, a Meskwaki artist, author, and educator, was the first Native American elected to the Iowa Women's Hall of Fame. Bertha Waseskuk, Meskwaki, was a historian and chronicler of Meskwaki history whose loss is still felt by the tribe. The contributions of all the indigenous women of Iowa deserve to be more widely known.

MESKWAKI

Name means: "Red Earth People"
Other names: Fox, Mesquakie, Sac and Fox of the
   Mississippi in Iowa
They call themselves: Meshkwakiuk, "Red Earth People"
Language spoken/language family: Meskwaki/Algonkian
Residence in Iowa: 1730 to today
Location today: Sac and Fox of the Mississippi in Iowa,
   Meskwaki Settlement near Tama, Iowa

☾ ☾ ☾

The Meskwaki and the Sauk are two different tribes, but they are often spoken of as the Sac and Fox because of their historical alliance.
Both nations were located in Wisconsin and Michigan before the
1700s. The Meskwaki are also known historically but erroneously as
the Fox because the first Meskwaki met by the French were of the
Fox clan.

Starting in the early 1700s the Meskwaki occasionally came into
Iowa. In a long series of wars, the French almost succeeded in destroying them in 1730, but they took refuge among the Sauk and created an alliance that would become known as the Sac and Fox.

The Meskwaki settled throughout eastern Iowa in the territory
of the Ioway, who received them with friendship. Some of the Meskwaki stayed near the lead mines (also known as the Mines of
Spain) of Dubuque to mine there, as had earlier tribes like the Ioway.
The Meskwaki maintained their independence and had peaceful relations with the Americans (unlike the Sauk), although the United
States insisted on dealing with them as the Sac and Fox. They were located in the Mississippi River area of northeast Iowa in 1731 and 1732;
from 1733 to 1739 their villages were on the lower Cedar, Iowa, and

Wapsipinicon rivers. They had a large village on the Wapsipinicon River from 1740 to 1765. The Meskwaki dominated most of eastern Iowa as far as the Des Moines River from 1773 to 1833.

In 1804, under dubious circumstances, a treaty signed in St. Louis established relations between the United States and a tribe designated as the Sauk and Fox. This was actually a small band of Sauk in Missouri who were coerced into signing a treaty that gave away all the lands of the Sauk in Illinois and the Meskwaki in Iowa. Despite the fact that in 1815 a treaty was signed with the "Fox," the United States continued to lump the Sauk and the Meskwaki together as the "Sac and Fox." The alliance eventually ended, but because the United States saw the tribes as a single entity, the defeat of Black Hawk in 1832 forced the sale of Meskwaki lands in Iowa, although none of them had been involved in the Sauk conflict in Illinois. From 1833 to 1842 the Meskwaki lived on the Des Moines and Iowa rivers, and then, from 1842 to 1845, they lived by the second Fort Des Moines in Des Moines.

By the 1840s, continuing white settlement dispossessed the Meskwaki of all their lands, and in 1846 they and the Sauk were relocated by the U.S. government to Kansas, on a reservation on the Osage River. Some Meskwaki families remained in Iowa by hiding out along the Iowa and Cedar rivers. In the 1850s, homesick, beset by disease, and dissatisfied by the lack of game, the Meskwaki in Kansas devised a plan to purchase lands in their old home in Iowa. Selling their horses to raise funds, they received permission from the Iowa General Assembly in 1856 to purchase land and to live along the Iowa River. The lands there are thus private property, a settlement rather than a reservation.

The Meskwaki continue to live today near Tama, named after a Meskwaki leader (some whites knew them as Tama Indians). A fiercely independent people, they exist and define their identity on their own terms. They are known legally, however, as the Sac and Fox of the Mississippi in Iowa because of the early treaties made with the United States.

Traditional Culture

The Meskwaki have been among the most conservative of tribes, successfully retaining much of their traditional culture when so many others have not. They follow a clan system that passes through the father to his children. Clans include the Bear and the Fox. This system, with its associated feasts and bundle ceremonies, is at the center of Meskwaki tradition and religion. Traditional Meskwaki religion is very private. The Meskwaki were notable warriors, having honed their abilities in the terrible French wars and the continuing warfare against the Sioux and Illinois. However, they were always friendly to the Americans.

Like other tribes in Iowa, the Meskwaki combined farming of crops like corn, beans, and squash with hunting deer and trapping furs to trade. The last buffalo hunt was in 1821; after that, buffalo herds disappeared from eastern Iowa.

Traditional Meskwaki lodges, called wickiups, are covered by bark or cattail mats. Although Meskwaki today live in typical modern houses, wickiups are still made for special purposes. The Meskwaki have dances and ceremonies throughout the year, but only a few are open to nontribal members. The most famous event open to visitors is the Meskwaki powwow, held in late summer. This is a chance to see Meskwaki in traditional regalia, doing selected dances, as well as a chance to buy food and craft items from vendors. The Meskwaki Casino is also an attraction that the visitor interested in contemporary culture should experience, as an element of change in a conservative community.

Famous Meskwaki

The Meskwaki are remembered in place-names all over Iowa, from famous chiefs of the 1800s like Poweshiek and Wapello to other leaders like Taiomah or Tama. Other leaders include Appanoose, Kishkekosh, Nesouaquoit, and Peahmuskah. Wakechai was a Meskwaki warrior who made a famous drawing which portrayed the many animals, birds, and fish upon which the Meskwaki depended for life.

A CLOSER LOOK
Traditional Ways of Life

The native nations of Iowa developed their ways of life in response to Iowa's natural environment: its weather, seasons, animals, plants, and minerals. Iowa is in a transitional zone between the open plains of the west and the eastern woodlands; it is a mosaic of hardwood forests, tallgrass prairies, and wetlands. This resulted in tribal lifestyles that were similarly mosaic and transitional, with characteristics belonging to both the Eastern Woodlands (such as bark lodges) and the Plains-culture areas (such as tipis).

Although there were differences in the cultures, histories, and traditions of the different tribes, there were also similarities. All the historic tribes within Iowa tended to settle in villages in river valleys and were dependent on a combination of hunting and farming. The cycle of activities followed throughout the year was intricately bound to the cycle of seasons. The following annual cycle was typical for most of Iowa's tribes from 1700 to 1850.

Spring

The yearly cycle began in April, when the tribe returned from smaller, dispersed winter camps to the riverside villages where they grew their crops. The large summer houses, oval or square in shape, were covered by bark, preferably elm, which was flexible and waterproof. They settled up their accounts with the white traders, selling the last of their furs. Some tribes would rebury those who had died during the winter, in the graveyards near the villages. They opened underground pits or caches where they had stored crops, including corn, from the previous fall harvest, holding a big feast to welcome the spring and to bid farewell to the dead. Women began to repair the lodges and crop fences and to clear the fields and prepare them for planting. Some types of edible greens and medicinal plants were also gathered; other types matured at other times during the year.

In May the crops were planted, and the tribe marked this major event with ceremony and prayer. A feast was accompanied by the national dances as well as the war dance, in preparation for the war season. During this time, young men courted young women, and marriages were arranged and made. When the first thunder was heard, the sacred bundles were opened, and the season of storytelling was over.

Summer

Summer was the season of hunting and of war, generally fought over hunting rights to defined territories. After the corn was planted, in about June, it was time for many to leave the village for about a month. The young men went on long-distance hunts for deer and buffalo and on war parties. Some of the older men and women went to mine lead. Others went to fish and to gather bulrushes for making mats. Only a few elderly men and women, as well as children, stayed to watch the crops.

In late July, everyone returned to the village. Some brought back dried meat and fish, and some brought completed mats. When the corn was about knee-high, it was time to hoe and dig up weeds. By this time, some of the beans and squash were ready, so people exchanged goods and had feasts until the corn was ripe. The young men were always restless, so they frequently headed out in small war parties to avenge the deaths of relatives or to guard claimed hunting grounds.

The summer buffalo hunt occurred in July, with the people moving as a great group out onto the plains to camp in buffalo-hide tipis. When the green corn was ready for roasting there was a great feast. This was a celebration accompanied by gambling, horse racing, and the great tribal ball games of lacrosse. In August, the women gathered cattails to make coarse mats used for floors and winter lodge coverings, while finely made bulrush mats were used for sleeping mats or storage. Some men fished for sturgeon.

Fall

September was the time of harvest. The best of the harvest was saved for seed, and the rest was either dried and prepared for storage in the cache pits or eaten in a great celebratory feast. The people then prepared to leave the summer villages for the winter hunting grounds. Traders arrived at the summer villages and were told where they could build their houses; they provided credit for needed items like firearms, ammunition, blankets, cloth, kettles, and the like against the furs that would be trapped that winter. As part of the agreement, the traders often stayed in the villages to watch over the old men and women who could no longer travel.

The people were packed and ready to move in October. They left the village in a single group to go to winter hunting areas in the interior of the state for the second tribal buffalo hunt of the year. There they broke into smaller groups in scattered camps for about two months so they could hunt over a larger area and have a better chance of success. The first snow or heavy frost caused the sacred bundles to be closed, and the season of storytelling began.

Winter

Beaver trapping began in November and continued through the winter until April. In December, as winter set in, the smaller camps gathered into larger camps in sheltered river valleys; these were used as bases for hunting and trapping. In January, the people hunted bears, waking them from hibernation in their dens and fighting them with knives or clubs. Traders came in late winter to get the furs, as well as to trade cloth and ammunition and to join in the feasting. Some also liked to go ice fishing.

As winter came to a close in March, the people split up again, agreeing to meet at a given spot in a month's time. Most of the group went to a sugar camp to make maple syrup and sugar. The young men continued to trap and hunt beaver, raccoon, and muskrat. Others went to the wetlands to hunt and net waterfowl on their great migrations. In April, all gathered at the designated spot, so they could return as a group to their villages and begin the yearly cycle once more.

SAUK

Name means: "People of the Outlet"
Other names: Sac, Saki, Sac and Fox
They call themselves: Osakiwuk, "People of the Outlet,"
    sometimes mistranslated as "Yellow Earth People"
Language spoken/language family: Sauk/Algonkian
Residence in Iowa: 1760 to 1836
Location today: Sac and Fox Nation of Missouri near
    Reserve, Kansas; Sac and Fox Nation near Stroud,
    Oklahoma

❨ ❨ ❨

There was no such tribe as the "Sac and Fox." The Sauk and the Meskwaki (known also as the Fox) are two different tribes. They are often spoken of as the Sac and Fox because of their historical alliance, especially since the 1804 treaty that caused them to lose most of their lands. Both nations were located in Michigan and Wisconsin before the 1700s.

The Sauk are usually mistranslated as being the Yellow Earth People as a companion set to the Meskwaki, the Red Earth People. But Meskwaki say that the Sauk name is really Osakiwuk, which means the People of the Outlet, because they lived on the mouth of a river when the Meskwaki met them.

The Sauk were pushed south from homelands in Wisconsin and Michigan in the 1700s by the French and Chippewa and formed an alliance with the Meskwaki. The Sauk were the closest allies of the Meskwaki during the period when the French attempted to destroy the Meskwaki, and both tribes often sought refuge in Iowa. One group of Sauk were noted in Iowa at the rapids north of present-day Keokuk in the late 1700s. Another group, mostly Sauk, settled in Illinois, while a group made mostly of Meskwaki settled in Iowa, in Ioway tribal territory. The Iowa River was the western boundary of Sauk territory in the 1800s.

The Sauk and Meskwaki groups of eastern Iowa would become known as the Sauk and Fox of the Mississippi. This was to distinguish the eastern group of Sauk and Meskwaki from the western Sauk and Fox of the Missouri, a large band of mostly Sauk who settled along the Missouri and Osage rivers in Missouri in the late 1700s.

In 1804, through a combination of alcohol and coercion, a few Sauk headmen living in Missouri were misled into signing a treaty with the United States that gave away all Sauk and Fox lands on both sides of the Mississippi. This naturally angered the Sauk and Meskwaki living in Iowa and Illinois along the tributaries of the river. The Sauk and Fox of the Mississippi moved farther into Iowa, where they fought the Sioux over territory there. One story told of a Sauk attack, led by Pashepaho and Black Hawk, on the Ioway town at Iowaville on the Des Moines River in about 1819, which destroyed at least part of the Ioway nation.

Encouraged by the Treaty of 1804, American squatters illegally seized the principal Sauk village on Rock Island, as well as the Meskwaki and Ioway lead mines at Dubuque. Sauk warrior Black Hawk led his band in resistance, in the Black Hawk War of 1832, which was fought primarily in Illinois. Because of his earlier alliance with the British and his resistance against American intrusions, his group was known as the British band. However, Black Hawk was defeated within a year by Americans assisted by Sioux and Winnebago.

In 1837, Sauk and Fox claims to Iowa lands were established by the mixed-blood Sauk leader Keokuk in debate with the Sioux and the Ioway. Keokuk based his claim on the concept of ownership through conquest rather than through aboriginal title. Of course, this idea was close to the hearts of the Americans. They thus chose to recognize Keokuk as the leader of both tribes in treaty-making, although he had no traditional right to authority even in his own Sauk tribe, let alone the Meskwaki.

Various bands of Sauk and Fox continued to settle all over Iowa from the early 1800s until the 1840s. The Sauk village of Appanoose was on the Des Moines River. Meanwhile, Keokuk and other compliant leaders continued making land cession treaties. Keokuk's last village was on the old site of the last Ioway town at Iowaville, where his Sauk lived until 1842.

After a series of treaties, both Sauk bands (the Missouri and Mississippi/British bands) were moved onto reserves in Kansas. After the Meskwaki/Fox contingent returned to Iowa, the remaining Sac and Fox of the Mississippi, mostly Sauk from Black Hawk's group, moved in 1869 from Kansas to Indian Territory, which eventually became Oklahoma. Most of the Sauk who remained in Kansas as the Sac and Fox of the Missouri were from Keokuk's group.

Traditional Culture

Sauk culture was very similar to Meskwaki culture, with an emphasis on clan membership, warrior associations, and warbundles. Subsistence patterns were also the same as those of other tribes in Iowa, with farming during the summer and smaller camps in winter.

Famous Sauk

Makataimeshekiakiak (Black Hawk) was not a chief, but he was a resolute war leader. His refusal to abandon his beloved village of Rock Island was based in part on the assurance of support by other tribes, but as soon as he made his stand, the other tribes backed out and some betrayed him. His final defeat led to the Black Hawk Treaty of 1832 and the ceding of much of eastern Iowa. Pashepaho (the Stabber) was the chief of the Sauk at that time. A mixed-blood orator named Keokuk, by his brilliant defense of Sauk land claims in Iowa and his friendship with the U.S. government, took over leadership of the tribe. Another leader in Kansas was Hardfish. Perhaps the most famous Sauk of modern times was the Olympic athlete Jim Thorpe, winner of gold medals in the pentathlon and decathlon in 1912.

A CLOSER LOOK
Indian History

Indian knowledge of historical events dates back many hundreds, or possibly thousands, of years before the coming of white settlers. Before white settlement, native peoples passed along their history through spoken traditions or oral history. With the coming of white settlers, another dimension to history was added through the written word of explorers, military, traders, missionaries, and settlers. Soon, tribes had individuals who used the written word to record their tribal histories.

Before 1700: Native Nations of Iowa

In the centuries before Columbus landed in the West Indies, Iowa was home to many native groups, spread throughout the state. These Late Prehistoric groups, classified by archaeologists based upon artifacts like pottery, were known as Great Oasis, Mill Creek, Glenwood, and Oneota. All seem to have been at least partially indigenous to Iowa, with Woodland culture roots. Some archaeological traits originated in other areas, such as a set of religious concepts from Mississippian cultures downriver.

No one knows for sure what these indigenous groups called themselves. Archaeologists associate the Oneota with the Chiwere Siouan like the Ioway, Otoe, Missouria, and Winnebago and the Glenwood with Caddoans like the Pawnee. The Great Oasis and Mill Creek seem to have left Iowa, merging with some Central Plains elements to become the Mandan, Hidatsa, and Arikara in the Dakotas. By the 1300s, Iowa was inhabited only by the ancestors of the Ioway, Otoe, and Missouria.

Why did they leave? During the 1300s and 1400s, climate changes stressed natural resources, increasing conflict between the various groups. The climate on the plains also became wetter from the 1450s through the 1500s, thus more favorable for agriculture. However, Columbus would land in the West Indies in 1492, and changes were coming.

The arrival of Europeans in the western hemisphere had an impact upon Iowa people well before white settlers came into the area. European contact with the eastern seaboard and Mexico had significant repercussions. Disease undoubtedly entered via the Mississippi River and the Great Lakes, decimating native groups. Survivors were often assimilated into larger tribes. Trade goods like rings and metal began to trickle in.

The first contact between whites and Indians in Iowa came in 1673, with the visit of the French explorers Marquette and Joliet to a refugee village of Illinois Indians near the mouth of the Des Moines River. The Illinois had fled there to avoid the depredations of the Iroquois from the east. The Beaver Wars far to the east caused many tribes to flee westward. In fact, those distant wars were the root cause of the movement into Iowa of the Sauk and Meskwaki from the east and the Sioux from the north.

1700–1800: Iowa as a Refuge from Eastern Wars

Conflicts like the French and Indian War, the Revolutionary War, the War of 1812, and intertribal wars and intrigues in the east, as well as the westward expansion of American settlers, pushed many tribes west from their original homes in eastern states into Iowa, beginning in the late 1670s. Thus began a domino effect that resulted in many of the intertribal wars in Iowa during the 1700s.

The 1700s and early 1800s were marked by terrible wars among the Sioux, Sauk, Meskwaki, Omaha, and Ioway for Iowa lands. Although the French and Indian War and the Revolutionary War were fought farther east, they also affected the tribes of Iowa, in that tribal alliances with the French, British, or Americans became the basis of intensified intertribal conflicts.

In the 1700s, after wars with the French and with other Indian tribes, the Sauk and Meskwaki moved from Michigan and Wisconsin into Iowa and Illinois. Some of the Sioux pressed south into Iowa from Minnesota, where they were in conflict with the Ojibwa. These movements pressed Iowa's smaller resident tribes, notably the Ioway and Otoe, further west and south. The Otoe left Iowa to settle in Nebraska, near the Pawnee; the Ioway stayed in southern Iowa until the 1830s. The Omaha also continued to use western Iowa's Loess Hills.

The Ojibwa, Kickapoo, Mascouten, and Potawatomi occasionally camped in eastern Iowa or raided resident tribes like the Ioway for war trophies or slaves to trade to the French. The Comanches and Plains Apaches also raided tribes in Nebraska and Iowa for slaves to trade to the Spanish in New Mexico.

The native nations of Iowa began to experience changes in culture also because of the expansion of the fur trade and the exchange of trade goods. For example, Iowa tribes ceased making pottery and stone tools as metal pots and tools became more available through white traders.

In the late 1700s, French settlements were established in a few places in eastern Iowa. Julien Dubuque arranged to mine lead with the Meskwaki and Ioway at the Mines of Spain (Iowa, at the time, was under Spanish control). Louis Tesson was awarded the first Spanish land grant in 1799. These early settlements and trade partnerships between Iowa tribes and European adventurers were additionally developed and strengthened through marriages and liaisons. The children of these unions were the earliest mixed-bloods.

1800–1900: War, Treaties, and Removal

Throughout the early 1800s, the wars in Iowa among the Sioux, the Sauk and Meskwaki, and the Ioway continued. In 1800, Spain transferred land, including Iowa, back to France. Three years later, the United States negotiated the Louisiana Purchase, including Iowa, from France. The explorations of newly acquired lands by Lewis and

Clark and by Zebulon Pike resulted in the first settlement of Iowa by Anglo-Americans.

The War of 1812 caused great intertribal friction as tribes like the Dakota sided with the United States; others such as the Sauk and Ioway were split between British and Americans, and still others like the Meskwaki tried to remain neutral. After the war, the treaty period began in earnest. Those tribes friendly to Americans were rewarded and the pro-British tribes were penalized.

As the U.S. frontier reached Iowa, conflicts such as the Black Hawk War of 1832 provided an opening to coerce the native nations of Iowa into a long series of treaties, from 1804 to 1857, ceding Iowa lands to the United States. In addition, the U.S. policy during the 1830s of removal of Indian tribes from homelands east of the Mississippi meant that many tribes were forcibly evicted to the newly designated Indian Territory, now Kansas and Oklahoma. The Neutral Ground was established in northeast Iowa, and some of the Winnebago were put there as a buffer between the Sauk and Meskwaki on the one side and the Sioux on the other between 1832 and 1846. After ceding traditional lands in Illinois and moving briefly to Missouri, a large band of the Potawatomi settled near Council Bluffs from 1833 to 1847.

The Spirit Lake Massacre of 1857 was a tragic incident between one desperate band of Wahpekute Santee Sioux and white squatters. This was just the prologue to the 1862 Dakota Uprising in Minnesota. After that, many Dakota were hanged in Minnesota and others were imprisoned at Davenport for a time.

Although tribes put up a spirited resistance, the native nations of Iowa were almost all moved between 1830 and 1860 onto reservations in Minnesota, Nebraska, the Dakotas, and Kansas. Even so, many returned to visit ancestral grounds and hunt when they could. Some families succeeded in living in small camps for decades longer when white communities were amenable, as in the case of Johnny Green's band of Potawatomi near Marshalltown or the Big Bears, a Winnebago family that lived in northeast Iowa.

Of all the native nations, only the Meskwaki understood enough of American ways to return to Iowa in 1856 to purchase a place with their own funds and with the agreement of the Iowa state government. Thus the Meskwaki Settlement, still existing near Tama, is not a reservation but the last remaining free community of any of Iowa's native nations.

Some members of the former tribes of Iowa, such as the Ioway and Otoe, fought in the Civil War on the side of the North. By the 1890s, only the Meskwaki remained in Iowa as a group, although members of the Yankton, Winnebago, and Omaha tribes continued to live as individuals in Iowa, especially in the area around Sioux City.

Some mixed-bloods married into white families, with the result that their descendants would know they were indeed part Indian but would know neither which tribe nor any cultural connection with their native roots. At the time it was an economic disadvantage and even dangerous to be recognizably Indian. Most mixed-bloods who could pass as white did so, often turning their backs on their Indian relatives in order to do better economically.

1900–Present: Endurance and Renewal

The Meskwaki stayed in Iowa on their settlement lands near Tama, preserving their traditions as well as adopting American ways to meet their needs. At the same time, Indians from out-of-state reservations like the Omaha, the Winnebago, and the Sioux continued to live and work in Iowa communities, such as Sioux City, throughout the 1900s, seeking jobs that were scarce at home on the reservations. Racism and poverty resulted in massive cultural and social damage for these people.

Indians from Iowa have served in World War I, World War II, the Korean War, the Vietnam War, the war in the Persian Gulf, and the wars in Afghanistan and Iraq. Indian veterans remain among the most respected people in their communities. Many know of the Navajo codetalkers of World War II; the Meskwaki also served as codetalkers in North Africa. Changes in federal policy, such as the Indian

Reorganization Act of 1934 and the Self-Determination Act, resulted in Indian communities having more say in their own future, including programs for employment, civil rights, education, and housing.

Today Sioux City, Des Moines, Council Bluffs, Davenport, Iowa City, and Cedar Rapids have substantial urban Indian populations. In addition, many of the colleges and universities in Iowa have attracted Indian students from areas all over the United States.

The political struggle for Indian rights was evident from several incidents in Iowa. The Omaha and Winnebago fought for reservation lands lost to Iowa through shifts in the channel of the Big Bend of the Missouri River. They won, and subsequently they put the first Indian casinos in Iowa on that land. The 1976 trial of two Indians involved with the American Indian Movement occupation of Wounded Knee was moved to Cedar Rapids, and they were acquitted. Sioux City has been a focus of the Indian struggle, thanks to a relatively high Indian population and discrimination there in housing and employment.

Many Iowans who have native blood from Indian groups throughout the United States have lost contact with their relatives and their roots through historical accident, although in some cases ancestors have rejected their Indian identity. Some may have a relatively high percentage of Indian blood, others much less; they may appear to be white or black but may self-identify as Indian. For many, a sense of identity is a large question mark in their lives.

The contemporary Indians of Iowa continue to make efforts to maintain their cultures and rights. Battles continue over such issues as discrimination and health, Indian gaming, and the protection of burial and archaeological sites. Another issue is the exploitation of Indian tradition through ignorance or fraud, especially through the commercialization of the popular interest in Indian art, traditions, and spirituality. It is important to remember that when it comes to Indian spirituality, one should never pay to pray. All of these issues are ones which generations to come must address with honesty and concern.

OMAHA AND PONCA

Omaha

Name means: "Upstream People"

Other names: Maha

They call themselves: Umáha, "Upstream People"

Language spoken/language family: Omaha (or Dhegiha)/ Siouan

Residence in Iowa: Prehistory to 1700, hunting rights through 1800s

Location today: Omaha Tribe of Nebraska near Macy, Nebraska

Ponca

Name means: Original meaning unknown

Other names: None

They call themselves: Panka

Language spoken/language family: Ponca (or Dhegiha)/ Siouan

Residence in Iowa: Prehistory, as part of the ancestral Omaha-Ponca

Location today: Ponca Tribe of Nebraska near Niobrara, Nebraska; Ponca Tribe of Oklahoma

❨ ❨ ❨

During their earliest migrations through Iowa, the ancestors of the Omaha and Ponca had not yet split into two separate peoples; thus they are considered together here. Their identities as separate tribes did not begin until their movement into South Dakota and Nebraska. According to some traditions, the ancestral Omaha-Ponca traveled north through Iowa along the Des Moines River or the Raccoon River. Archaeologists differ in their interpretations as to which archaeological culture best represents ancestral Omaha-Ponca, some proposing the Oneota and others the Glen Elder culture. One of the early Omaha sites is at Blood Run, a precontact intertribal trading center in northwest Iowa which they and the Ioway-Otoe occupied until about 1700, when the Yankton Sioux took over the area. Buffalo hides and pipestone were the primary trade interests.

After about 1700, the Omaha-Ponca moved into South Dakota and Nebraska. One group moved off and became the Ponca, who stayed north in South Dakota and Nebraska and adopted many Plains traits through their close contact with the Sioux. In comparison, the Omaha adopted a more sedentary lifestyle centered on their gardens and earthlodge villages, adopted from the Arikara whom they met on their westward journey. Both Omaha and Ponca became true Plains peoples, usually at war with neighbors like the Lakota. By the 1770s the Omaha were firmly established in Nebraska, but they retained hunting rights in western Iowa through the early pioneer period. The Ponca consider the Niobrara River region in Nebraska to be their homeland.

A treaty signed in 1854 established the Omaha reservation, which was allotted—divided into small subsistence plots—in 1882 by the Omaha Allotment Act. Local histories assert that some Omaha individuals still used lands in western Iowa through the early part of the twentieth century. In the Fort Laramie Treaty of 1868, Ponca lands were inadvertently assigned to the Sioux. They were then further ordered to move to Indian Territory in Oklahoma in 1876; they resisted but were forced to move. A group of thirty Ponca led by Chief Standing Bear headed home in 1879 in defiance of the U.S. government and were arrested. Chief Standing Bear tried to return from Oklahoma to rebury his son in ancestral lands in Nebraska. The trial of Standing Bear in 1879 has national significance as the first time an American court recognized Indians as "persons within the meaning of the law" who have rights of citizenship. The trial also established the right of the Ponca to stay in their Niobrara homelands; however, their lands had already been reassigned. The southern Ponca stayed in Oklahoma. This event resulted in the separation of the Ponca into the Northern Ponca Tribe of Nebraska and the Ponca Tribe of Oklahoma.

During the 1970s, the Omaha reasserted their claim over Blackbird Bend, which was originally their land in Nebraska but which, because of a shift in the course of the Missouri River, had become part of Iowa. The dispute went to the Supreme Court, where the Omaha were successful. This land was later used for the establishment of the tribal casino.

In 1962, the United States terminated the federal status of the Ponca of Nebraska. The termination was finally reversed in 1992 after continuing efforts by the tribe. Today they own land in Nebraska, but it is not a reservation. In 1994 the two branches joined in a powwow on their Nebraska lands, with the southern Ponca helping their northern kin reestablish many of their cultural ways. Thus the Ponca are once again united, in identity if not politically.

The Omaha and Ponca speak dialects of the same language, known to linguists as Dhegiha, along with three other tribes, the Osage, Kansa, and Quapaw. Omaha and Ponca are mutually intelligible, although native speakers note significant differences.

Traditional Culture

In 2000, it was estimated that there were about forty native speakers of Omaha left, although the tribe had begun an active program to preserve the language; fewer than twenty-five speakers of Ponca were left at the time.

The Omaha and Ponca social systems were based on clan membership that passed through the father, usually associated with some symbolic animal.

The Omaha recalled that their ancestors had used bark lodges, but by the 1800s they lived in villages of earthlodges, like the Pawnee, Arikara, and Mandan. During buffalo hunts they used tipis. The more nomadic Ponca lived primarily in tipis while on the move but also had earthlodge villages.

The Omaha are most famous among other tribes for their pow-wow dancing, through the ancient Hethushka warrior society, as it is known today. The Omaha have experienced a cultural revival in recent years, based on the preservation of their language and the recovery of their Sacred Pole and Sacred Hide, sacred tribal items. They are also active and progressive in reburial programs. The Ponca are also reconnecting and rebuilding their traditional culture.

Famous Omaha and Ponca

Blackbird was a controversial chief of the Omaha during the early contact period, and through his influence the Omaha rose to their greatest prominence. Big Elk was a later, well-regarded chief. Francis La Flesche was a mixed-blood who helped record Omaha culture; his daughter Susan La Flesche Picotte, the first Indian woman to become a physician, worked tirelessly for Indian rights and health. Of course the most famous of all was Standing Bear, the Ponca patriot whose trial ensured that all Indian people were recognized as human beings.

A CLOSER LOOK
Native Spirituality

Traditional Indian spirituality was closely tied to accepted norms within the family, clan, and tribe and was based upon connections to ancestors and traditional territory. Native spirituality was not concerned with converting others; it was specific within the group. Within one's lineage, there was a strict covenant between the people, the Creator, and the spiritual forces of the land.

The center of religious life was the clan, which for most tribes in Iowa was traced through the father. Depending on the tribe, clans were generally identified with animals like the bear, wolf, fox, or buffalo or through other natural elements, such as thunder. Clan religious life was centered on ceremonies, feasts, and rituals and one or more sacred bundles. Bundles were like portable altars and were handed down for generations. Inside were materials used in the ceremonies, such as whistles, pipes, and war amulets.

It was usual for a boy to seek a vision before he entered puberty, to gain from animals and other spirits special spiritual help in war, healing, or other tasks. He would blacken his face with charcoal, go to an isolated spot, and wander about alone, fasting. This activity was dangerous, not only because of enemy tribes but because not all spirits were good or friendly.

The Creator gave tobacco to native people for specific use in prayer. Only native tobacco was used, sometimes mixed with dogwood or willow bark shavings. No other substances were used in pipes. Smoking was communion with Creator, prayers in one's breath mingled with the smoke, which was pleasing to the spirits.

Another ancient rite was that of the sweatlodge, used for purification and healing. In some ways the sweatlodge was like a sauna, a small covered lodge where water was poured over very hot rocks to produce steam. Extremely hot, in a small dark space, and accompanied with prayers and songs, the experience was felt to be like being reborn from the womb. Traditionally, men and women used the sweatlodge separately.

Besides the clans, there were other associations such as warrior societies, each with its own dress, rules, and songs. The tribes of Iowa did not perform the Sun Dance, a Plains ceremony; rather, their main tribal ceremony was the Medicine Dance. This secret ceremony in a long lodge centered on the use of adoption, initiation, and feats of spiritual power such as "shooting" each other with invisible "darts" from otterskin bags. Originating among the Ojibway, it was most popular among Iowa's tribes during the 1700s and 1800s. Another ceremony was the Drum Dance or Dream Dance, not to be confused with the popular powwow. However, the powwow does carry spiritual significance for many people today.

Many have heard of the Native American Church, in which peyote, a type of cactus from Texas and Mexico, is used. Peyote is not smoked but is most commonly eaten as a button or powder or drunk as tea. It usually makes participants throw up impurities, and visions can come but not always. It is mostly a medicine for healing, especially effective against alcohol, but it is traditionally used only within a proper all-night ceremonial context, in a group, with a special form of water drum, rattle, and singing. It is treated very seriously by native people.

Today, native spirituality is still connected to ancestral bloodlines and sacred places. However, many of the larger tribal celebrations are no longer held, and traditions are often carried on privately within the family. Many families combine elements of traditional spirituality with Christian worship. Still, the connections must be maintained with the tribal community.

Some families still pray with tobacco and pipe or cigarette, participate in clan or healing ceremonies, use the sweatlodge, attend Native American Church meetings, and reconnect through powwows. These ways are held sacred and private, shared only with family members and the closest of friends. They are never for display.

Unlike Christianity, Indian religion was never about conversion or attracting new believers. The Creator had given each tribe its own set of laws and beliefs, which that tribe accepted as a covenant for itself only. Also, while elders were respected and looked to for guidance, ultimately every person made his or her own relationship with God. The Indian way was to follow the rules of the community and when necessary go right to the source—the ancestors, the land, and the Creator.

Often through dissatisfaction with their own churches and a desire for spiritual consolation, many non-Indians look toward Indians for answers. In some ways, the sharing has been good. In other ways, the unknowledgeable have been taken advantage of by individuals who represent themselves as teachers or spiritual leaders but who are really trying to gain influence or make a quick profit.

If you are interested in learning about native spirituality, keep several important points in mind. One important red flag is a fee for spirituality. Real spiritual leaders are so busy and tied down to their own communities' needs that they don't have time to go on a speaker's circuit or give regular workshops.

If you meet people claiming to teach native spirituality in Iowa, ask which tribe they purport to represent, and contact that tribe for the truth. It is a generally accepted practice in Indian country to give your lineage, whom you learned from, and which tribe you are part of. Check up on someone you just met. Was that tribe historically connected to Iowa? Native spirituality is always tied to specific tribes and their homelands. Most books on native spirituality, even in the Native American section of a bookstore, should be considered works of imagination rather than truth, even if the author has an Indian-sounding name. A few books are good starting points, and those are recommended at the end of this book.

Perhaps the best way to begin to learn about real Indian ways is to attend a powwow, especially those held on reservations or Indian communities, such as at the Meskwaki Settlement or the Omaha

Reservation. Powwows do charge admission these days, and that is legitimate. Most important, realize that these are private occasions, shared rarely. Perhaps the best thing you can do if you are interested in native ways is to reconnect to your own family, to your own ancestors, and to the land you call home. That is exactly what the native way is about.

OTOE AND MISSOURIA

Otoe
Name means: "People of This Place"
Other names: Oto, Otoe-Missouria
They call themselves: Jiwere, "Arrived at the Place" or
    "People of This Place"
Language spoken/language family: Chiwere Siouan
Residence in Iowa: Prehistory to 1750s, hunting into 1830s
Location today: Otoe-Missouria Tribe near Red Rock,
    Oklahoma

Missouria
Name means: "Dwellers on the River"
Other names: Missouri, Otoe-Missouria
They call themselves: Nyiudachi, "Dwellers on the River"
Language spoken/language family: Chiwere Siouan
Residence in Iowa: Prehistory to about 1798, hunting into 1830s
Location today: Otoe-Missouria Tribe near Red Rock,
    Oklahoma

☾ ☾ ☾

Originally, the Otoe and the Missouria were two distinct tribes. Decimation of the Missouria in the early 1800s caused them to join the Otoe. The name Otoe was historically derived from Wat'odatan, a name used by the related Missouria and Ioway to tease them because of an affair between an Otoe man and a Missouria woman. But the Otoe call themselves Jiwere, translated as "Arrived at the Place" or "People of This Place."

The Otoe were recorded by French explorers as being in Iowa, in the Des Moines River area, from about 1690 to 1700. The Otoe, the

Missouria, the Ioway, and the Winnebago show up in the prehistoric record as the Oneota culture. The Otoe lived near the Ioway during both tribes' earliest histories, the Otoe being especially connected to the Blue Earth area and southwestern Iowa. After leaving Iowa by the 1750s, they crossed the Missouri River to Nebraska. Along with other tribes, they continued to use western Iowa as hunting grounds into the mid 1800s.

The Missouria's name, Nyiudachi, has been translated many ways, but all have to do with the river, such as "Dwellers on the River" or "Floating Dead down the River" or "Came down the River."

The Missouria nation lived along the stretch of the Missouri from its junction with the Mississippi to southwestern Iowa. The Missouri River was named after the Missouria by French explorers. A series of disastrous wars with neighboring tribes, over diminishing resources and lands, ended with their near-annihilation by the Sauk and Meskwaki in about 1798. Most of the survivors sought refuge among the Otoe, although some also went among the Kansa, Osage, and other tribes.

Living in villages along the Platte River in Nebraska by 1750, the Otoe and Missouria still retained hunting rights in western Iowa. After ceding their lands in Nebraska in 1854, the Otoe and Missouria were assigned the Big Blue River Reservation on the Kansas-Nebraska border. After their lands there were sold without their consent in the 1880s, they bought their own reservation with their own money in Oklahoma; this land was subsequently allotted, most of it passing out of their hands. Now classified as one tribe, they are called the Otoe-Missouria of Oklahoma, with communities near Red Rock, Oklahoma, where the tribal offices are located.

Traditional Culture

Otoe and Missouria traditional culture was very much like that of the Ioway, as they had all shared a common past. Tribal life was based on the clan system, led by the Bear and Buffalo clans, with others such as the Beaver, Owl, and Eagle. The pipe bundle was the center of clan religious life. However, when the Otoe moved from Iowa to Nebraska, they located near the Pawnee and had more exposure to the open Plains lifestyle than did the Ioway. Thus the Otoe adopted the earthlodge and other Plains traits that were not noted among the Ioway. They were skilled buffalo hunters and farmers. Though joined politically, the Missouria families have kept some degree of cultural distinctiveness, such as the use of particular clan rights and names, until the present time.

Famous Otoe and Missouria

Some famous Otoe from the contact period were Chief Shaumo-nekusse (also called the Prairie Wolf or L'Ietan), his wife, Hayne Hudjihini, and Chiefs Shunkapi, White Horse, and Nowaykesugga. Truman Dailey was an Otoe-Missouria who dedicated himself to language and culture preservation. Anna Lee Walters, Otoe-Pawnee, is a noted writer.

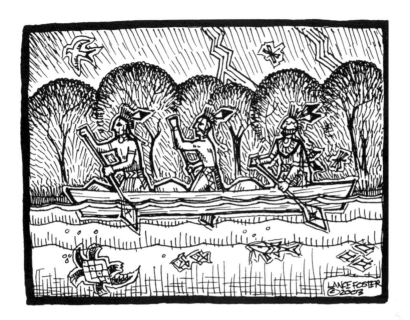

A CLOSER LOOK
Languages and Place-Names

There is no such thing as "the Indian language." Each native nation had its own language. Some were similar, such as Potawatomi and Meskwaki or Dakota and Ioway. Others were totally different from each other, such as Pawnee and Omaha.

Indian languages originally had no written form. When white explorers tried to write them down, many variations were created, even for the same name. In some cases, agreement was finally achieved, but not always.

Linguists have grouped together a number of languages like Winnebago, Ioway, Osage, and Omaha as Siouan, because of their similarity to the most famous languages spoken by the Sioux, Lakota, Dakota, and Nakota.

There were hundreds of Indian languages in North America, some as different from each other as English and Chinese. In Iowa, at least five different Indian languages were spoken at various times, most of them belonging to two language families, Siouan and Algonquian. Some of them were spoken here for centuries (Ioway and Oto) and some for a year or less (Huron). The following list provides the major language families and the languages belonging to them.

SIOUAN FAMILY: Dakota (Santee), Nakota (Yankton Sioux), Chiwere (Ioway-Otoe-Missouria), Winnebago (Hochunk), Dhegiha (Omaha-Ponca)

ALGONQUIAN FAMILY: Meskwaki-Sauk, Kickapoo-Mascouten, Illinois, Miami-Wea, Potawatomi-Ottawa-Ojibwa

CADDOAN FAMILY: Pawnee, Arikara

IROQUOIAN FAMILY: Huron (also known as Wyandot)

To give an idea of the differences and similarities among these languages, here are a few examples:

LANGUAGE	SUN	WATER	BUFFALO	MAN	HOUSE
Ioway	bi	nyi	che	wanye	chi
Winnebago	wira	ni	che	wak	chi
Omaha	bi	ni	te	shenu	ti
Dakota	wi	mni	pte	wicasa	ti
Meskwaki	kisheswa	nepi	kobichi	neni	wikiup
Potawatomi	kises	mbish	pkocshuke'	nIne	wigwam
Illinois	kiilhswa	nipi	irenanswa	iriniwa	wiikiaami
Arikara	shakuúnu	tstooxo	tanaha	wiita	akaanu
Pawnee	shakuúno	kiicu	taraha	piita	akaaru

Many Iowans are familiar with Indian words through place-names in the state. The name of the state itself, which is said to be an Indian word meaning anything from "The Beautiful Land" to "This Is the Place," was actually taken from the Iowa River, named for the Ioway Indians who lived along it. Defining Iowa as meaning "The Beautiful Land" in some mysterious "Indian language" might have been more appealing to settlers seeking a new start than a reference to the original people—who were removed from their lands before most American settlers entered Iowa.

Many rivers, such as the Wapsipinicon, have retained their original native names, although some have been translated into English, as with the Raccoon and (Smells-Like-)Skunk rivers. Some places are named for the native nations themselves, like the state of Iowa, Sioux City, and Potawatomi County, or for Indian leaders such as Decorah (Winnebago), Keokuk (Sauk), Winneshiek (Winnebago), Poweshiek (Meskwaki), Black Hawk (Sauk), Mahaska (Ioway), and War Eagle (Yankton Sioux). These names all reflect real historical connections to the native nations of Iowa.

Other places, such as Osceola and Cherokee, were named by American settlers for Indian tribes or leaders who never lived in Iowa, perhaps because of romantic ideas or nostalgia for home states back east. Still other places have names which have no meaning in any Indian language but were invented by white settlers, such as Keomah.

PAWNEE AND ARIKARA

Pawnee
Name means: Original meaning unknown; comes from
    Siouan referring to unrelated peoples to the west
Other names: Pani, Panimaha
They call themselves: No separate term for themselves as a
    whole; used the names of their four bands
Language spoken/language family: Pawnee/Caddoan
Residence in Iowa: Prehistory, hunting into 1830s
Location today: Pawnee Tribe near Pawnee, Oklahoma

Arikara
Name means: Original meaning unknown
Other names: Arickaree, Ree
They call themselves: Sahnish, "Human Being"
Language spoken/language family: Arikara/Caddoan
Residence in Iowa: Prehistory
Location today: Fort Berthold Indian Reservation, New
    Town, North Dakota; Three Affiliated Tribes near New
    Town, North Dakota

《 《 《

The Pawnee and Arikara were part of the Caddoan peoples who in prehistoric times moved from the south and west, especially Nebraska, into Iowa, bringing with them their earthlodge house types, pottery making, and corn horticulture. In Iowa, they are associated with the archaeological cultures of Glenwood and the Coalescent Tradition. As late as 1200 there were Arikara or Pawnee villages in southwest Iowa. By 1550, the Arikara had moved up the Missouri River to new villages in central South Dakota.

The Pawnee, historically residents of Nebraska, were made up of four bands. The Arikara, historically residents of South and North Dakota, are associated with Iowa primarily through prehistoric sites, such as Glenwood and Blood Run. The Pawnee used southwest Iowa as hunting grounds and even had small villages or camps there into the early 1800s. In 1862, the Arikara joined the Mandan and Hidatsa at Like-a-Fishhook Village in North Dakota, together forming the Three Affiliated Tribes. The Pawnee were forced from Nebraska by the United States and resettled in Oklahoma, where they live today.

Traditional Culture

Originally there was no name for the four bands as a group; each band was known by its own name. There are four distinctive groups: the Ckiri (Skiri, Skidi, Panimaha, or Pawnee Loups or Wolves); the Cawi'i (Chawi or Grand Pawnee); the Kitkahahki (Republican Pawnee); and the Pitahawirata (Tappage Pawnee).

The Arikara and Pawnee developed a complex religious system which influenced many of their Siouan neighbors, including the Omaha, Otoe, Ioway, and, to a lesser extent, the Dakota. While the Omaha are the originators of the Plains powwow with their Omaha Dance, the roots of that dance are in the Pawnee Iruska ceremonial. The greatest intertribal ceremonial of adoption and of making the relationships vital for peace and trade, the Pipe Dance, is said to have come from the Caddoan tribes, with some traditions indicating that the transfer occurred at the Blood Run site on the Big Sioux River in northwest Iowa and southeast South Dakota.

Corn was at the heart of the Arikara and Pawnee religion. They were expert horticulturalists, growing corn, beans, and squash, and they hunted buffalo. They lived in earthlodge villages and used tipis while on the buffalo hunt.

Famous Pawnee

One of the most famous Pawnee was Petalasharo, who stopped the age-old sacrifice to the Morning Star through a heroic rescue of the victim in the middle of the ceremony. Another notable Pawnee chief was Sharitarish. The Echohawk family of today are national leaders in Indian rights.

Among the notable Arikara are Bloody Knife, who was a scout for Custer, and Bloody Hound, who was chief when artist George Catlin visited the tribe in the 1830s.

A CLOSER LOOK
Archaeology in Iowa

Iowans are usually most familiar with the native nations of Iowa through archaeology. Collections of artifacts found while farming are common. Arrowheads, knives, pottery fragments or shards, bannerstones, grinding stones . . . people enjoy these tangible pieces of a long-vanished way of life. Artifacts are important for the story they tell about the time period in which they were made and used. When they are removed from a site, most of their story is lost. While collections of tools are attractive, out of context they are like pages torn from a book. Many important sites have been destroyed in the search for curiosities, although to a lesser extent today than in the past.

Out of curiosity or scientific interest, early travelers and scientists often excavated Indian graves, not only ancient ones but even recent burials of people whose relatives were still mourning. The robbery of the body of Black Hawk was discovered by his wife when she came to visit his grave. Indians were treated as curiosities rather than as human beings. The legacy of grave robbing and casual treatment by white collectors has created bad feelings in Indians that persist to this day.

In 1971, Maria Pearson of the Yankton Sioux learned of road-building activities that were destroying a cemetery. White remains were reburied, but Indian remains from the same period were collected and shipped to Iowa's Office of the State Archaeologist. A long fight by Pearson and her allies helped people understand the racism inherent in this unequal treatment of the dead. In 1976, Iowa was the first state to pass a law protecting burials, no matter what the race of the deceased. This was the forerunner to similar laws in other states, as well as to the Native American Graves Protection and Repatriation Act of 1990. Today, in a spirit of respect and cooperation,

Indians and archaeologists are learning from each other in partnership. One of the most important national cultural-preservation laws today had its beginning in Iowa.

Iowa's Office of the State Archaeologist is the best contact for those interested in archaeology in Iowa. The OSA helps coordinate local archeological interest groups in the state through the Iowa Archeological Society, which sponsors local events and publishes a journal.

Those truly concerned about our past would do well to consider the following advice. Buying and selling artifacts supports a trade that destroys our past. Collecting artifacts on federal and other public lands is illegal. Collections acquired on one's own land are legal, but information is lost in the process. Much more can be gained by leaving artifacts in place and becoming involved with Iowa's archaeological groups to discover how best to be a steward of the sites in your care.

11,000–8500 B.C.: Ancient Hunters
The PaleoIndian Period (Over 13,000 to 10,500 years ago)

ENVIRONMENT: The PaleoIndians lived in a moist, cool landscape very different from the one we know today. Recently emerged from its glacial covering, the land was scarred from the action of the ice, scraped flat except for odd hills and ridges left behind in its wake. Scattered across the countryside were lakes and marshes, creeks, rivers, and springs. Stands of coniferous and birch forests in the north gave way to elm and oak in the south. Herds of mammoth, mastodon, giant long-horned bison, and caribou roamed the landscape.

CULTURE: Bands of PaleoIndian families followed the big game. In the earliest phases they hunted mammoth and mastodon, but as those fell into extinction they switched to huge long-horned bison. Most of their diet was meat, supplemented with smaller game, eggs, and wild plants. The population was small and traveled constantly, probably living in brush shelters in the warmer seasons and in skin shelters in colder weather.

ARTIFACTS: The Clovis point, the Folsom point (both named for their provenance), and the Gainey point (apparently transitional between the first two) are diagnostic artifacts for this period. The points were fluted, which means they had long dished-out areas along each flat side. They were highly finished and wonderfully crafted. Later in the PaleoIndian period, smaller unfluted points appeared, of the Dalton, Fayette, Agate Basin, and Hell Gap types.

SITES IN IOWA: Over two hundred early PaleoIndian points have been found in uplands and river valleys on the surface or along streams as isolated discoveries, where erosion by wind or water has uncovered them. The Rummells-Maske site, where a cache of over twenty Clovis points was found, is along the Cedar River in eastern Iowa. It is the only early PaleoIndian site excavated in Iowa so far.

8500–800 B.C.: Hunters and Gatherers
The Archaic Period (10,500 to 2,800 years ago)

ENVIRONMENT: The Archaic was a period of radical change in the environment from the earlier PaleoIndian period. The glacial landscape of tundra and evergreens was becoming covered in deciduous forests, although some open prairie remained in the western part of Iowa. The biggest animals, like the mammoth, could not survive the changes and became extinct. From 5,500 to 2,500 years ago, during a climatic episode called the Atlantic or Hypsithermal, the climate became very warm and dry.

CULTURE: With the extinction of the megafauna, Indians of the Archaic period switched to smaller game, like deer and elk, and began to use more wild plants for food. Some also relied on fish and freshwater clams. People lived in base camps but traveled to outlying locations where different plant sources could be located seasonally.

During the warmer and drier Hypsithermal period, communities moved from upland areas down into the river valleys to be closer to water. In western Iowa, buffalo provided the greater part of the diet, while in eastern Iowa the Indians explored a wider range of plant and animal resources, including those from wetlands. Populations grew and became more attached to specific places.

ARTIFACTS: Tools included stemmed and notched medium to large points. Later in the period, smaller points and bannerstones (ground-stone weights) marked the arrival of the atlatl, or spear-thrower. Stone was also shaped through smoothing and grinding; tools made in this manner are called ground-stone tools. Most of these tools were used to grind seeds and plants into foods and medicines. Other ground-stone tools included axes, net weights, manos (grinding stones held in the hand), and metates (the base stone against which the mano grinds the seeds). Fish hooks made from bone have also been found. At the Cherokee Sewer site was found a bone whistle, one of the oldest musical instruments of its type ever found in North America. The increasing variety of tools reveals how people were learning more and more about different foods and other resources that could be gathered and processed.

SITES IN IOWA: Unfortunately, from an archaeological viewpoint, the Hypsithermal was a time of accelerated erosion, as dry masses of silt gradually washed down into the river valleys over hundreds of years. These colluvial deposits slowly buried camp remains, often to a depth of a hundred feet or more, making sites from this period difficult to locate. Important sites in Iowa from the Archaic include the Cherokee Sewer site near Cherokee, Turkey River Mounds near Guttenberg, the Turin site near Turin, the Simonsen site south of Cherokee, and the Gast Spring site near Grandview. Most of these sites cannot be visited without making arrangements with landowners. If interested, contact Iowa's Office of the State Archaeologist. The Turkey River Mounds site near Guttenberg is open for visitation, but please respect the site and do not remove any artifacts.

800 B.C.–A.D. 1000: Farmers, Traders, and Moundbuilders
The Woodland Period (2,800 to 1,000 years ago)

ENVIRONMENT: The transition from the Hypsithermal to the Woodland period was marked by increased rainfall. The environment became wetter and more humid, more like the Iowa we know today. The term "Woodland" is used because related cultures covered a large part of the woodlands of the eastern and midwestern United States.

CULTURE: Indians began to stay in defined areas and develop local cultures based on the rich resources of those areas. The bow and arrow replaced the atlatl. Some groups began to experiment with growing squash, sunflowers, amaranth, chenopodium, and eventually corn and beans. Shelters were varied, but the bark lodge was probably the most typical. During the Middle Woodland period, a great trading network called the Hopewell Interaction Sphere stretched across much of America, including Iowa, with trade in obsidian and grizzly claws from the Rocky Mountains, copper from the Great Lakes, and seashells from the Gulf Coast. This was the most active period of mound building in Iowa. Elaborate grave goods such as beads and pottery were often placed with burials. During the Late Woodland period, the trading network shrank. The Effigy Mounds of northeast Iowa, so called because they are in the shapes of bears, birds, and other animals, were built during this last period and may have marked the territories of clan groups.

ARTIFACTS: The Woodland period has perhaps the widest variety of projectile points and blades of all Iowa archaeological periods. Typical forms were notched on the corners or had stems. Some forms are quite spectacular and large and may represent not arrow or spear points but knives. There are also smaller points popularly known as bird points. Birds were actually hunted with sharpened arrow shafts, feathered but without stone points, or were caught in traps or nets. Stone was ground or abraded in various forms with the three-quarter grooved-style ax probably used for woodworking and felling trees. It was during the Woodland period that people first began to make pottery of many different styles in Iowa. Most mixed sand grit with clay to keep the pots from breaking during firing. A common decorative technique called for pressing twine and other woven fiber in patterns into the wet clay pot before it was fired.

SITES IN IOWA: Many Woodland sites, including mounds, are open to the public in Iowa. Some of them include Effigy Mounds National Monument near Harper's Ferry, Toolesboro Mounds near Toolesboro, Little Maquoketa River Mounds and the Mines of Spain near Dubuque, Turkey River Mounds near Guttenberg, Pikes Peak State Park near McGregor, Palisades-Kepler State Park near Mount Vernon, Fish Farm Mounds near New Albin, Slinde Mounds near Waukon, Lacey-Keosauqua State Park near Keosauqua, Malchow Mounds near Kingston, Ledges State Park near Boone, and Dolliver Memorial State Park and Vegors Cemetery near Lehigh. Many of these sites are considered sacred and some contain burials. Visitors should behave respectfully as they would in any cemetery.

A.D. 1000–1650: Villagers and Warriors
Late Prehistoric Period (1,000 to 350 years ago)

ENVIRONMENT: During the Late Prehistoric period, sometimes known as the Post-Woodland period, the environment was much the same as it is today. There were some slight variances, such as during the Little Ice Age, a cooling period of extended winters and cool summers.

CULTURE: Settlements were more substantial and inhabited for longer time periods. Farming was more established by this time, and corn, beans, pumpkins, and squash became staples. Storage pits in the ground were used to keep foods and belongings safe while people were away on hunting trips. Moundbuilding declined as people favored burial in level cemeteries, although the Oneota seem occasionally to have placed burials in mounds.

This period is marked by the development of at least four distinct cultures in Iowa: Great Oasis, Mill Creek, Glenwood, and Oneota. Differentiated according to house form, settlement pattern, and pottery style, these cultures appear to have developed from earlier local Woodland cultures. Each culture had its own artifacts, way of life, and territory, which makes this perhaps the most complex of Iowa's archaeological periods.

The Great Oasis culture has features of both the Central Plains tradition and the Middle Missouri tradition. It is located in southern Minnesota, northwest Iowa, and central Iowa along the middle part of the Des Moines River and the lower part of the Raccoon River. The few houses known in Iowa were similar to Mill Creek lodges but were not fortified.

The Mill Creek culture of the Middle Missouri tradition is located in northwest Iowa along the Missouri, Big Sioux, and Little Sioux rivers. The houses were long, rectangular structures of timber and mud plaster, probably with gabled roofs. The medium-size villages were often protected by wooden palisades, ditches, and low earthen walls.

The Glenwood culture of the Central Plains tradition is located in eastern Nebraska and western Iowa in the Missouri River Valley and its tributaries. Glenwood culture sites are marked by small, unfortified villages of square earthlodges.

The Oneota culture of the Upper Mississippian tradition was centered in the Upper Mississippi River basin in Wisconsin, Minnesota, and Iowa; scattered sites occur in neighboring states. Oneota settlements were numerous in river valleys throughout Iowa. Bark- or mat-covered longhouses in villages that were often quite large were characteristic of the Oneota. The Oneota culture continued to exist in Iowa as the Ioway and Otoe tribes. In other states, the Oneota continued as the Winnebago and the Missouria. Some scholars believe other tribes may have also been involved at various times. No one is sure which tribes came from the Great Oasis or Mill Creek culture in Iowa; they may have been absorbed into other tribes. The Nebraska culture was possibly affiliated with the Pawnee or Arikara.

ARTIFACTS: Arrowheads, among the smallest types of projectile points, were often triangular during this period. They are sometimes called bird points by collectors, although birds were either trapped or shot with sharpened arrow shafts without stone points. Stone celts were ground and polished to be used as ax heads or war clubs. Tools for farming included hoes made from elk or bison shoulder blades and rakes made from deer antlers. The diagnostic pottery forms identify the different cultures of this period. Great Oasis pottery lacked handles and was finely crafted with sand or grit temper and incised decorations. Mill Creek pottery was globular in form with decorated rims and sometimes with handles; the upper portions of the sides were decorated with incised lines and geometric designs. Glenwood pottery was also globular, sometimes with small handles and most often with decorated rims and smooth sides. Oneota pottery, tempered with crushed shells, had handles and intricate designs of dots and lines that trailed over the entire vessel. During the latter part of this period, entering Protohistoric times, some of these cultures were no longer evident in Iowa, having moved away or been absorbed by other cultures such as the Oneota.

SITES IN IOWA: Late Prehistoric sites in Iowa include Glenwood, Blood Run National Historic Landmark near Rock Rapids, Wittrock Indian Village National Historic Landmark near Sutherland, and Hartley Fort in northeast Iowa. Special arrangements must be made with landowners to visit these sites.

A.D. 1650–1750: Traditions and Trade Goods
Protohistoric Period (350 to 250 years ago)

ENVIRONMENT: Woodlands extended along rivers throughout Iowa and also covered large areas of eastern Iowa. The rest of Iowa was mostly tallgrass prairie, with large areas of wetlands covering the north central part of the state, known today as the Des Moines lobe. Buffalo roamed throughout Iowa, especially in the drier portions of the western prairies. Elk, deer, and smaller game were plentiful. Iowa looked every bit a wilderness as Alaska does today.

CULTURE: By the start of this period, the other Late Prehistoric cultures had given way to the descendants of the Oneota, the Ioway, and the Otoe. Related Siouan-speaking tribes like the Missouria, Winnebago, Kansa, Omaha, and Ponca shared hunting territories in western Iowa. The Yankton and Dakota Sioux also ventured south into Iowa from their homelands in Minnesota. Refugee tribes from the east occasionally made incursions into Iowa. It was probably during this period that the tribes of Iowa first acquired horses, as well as trade goods such as metal knives and pots and glass beads and bottles. This was the beginning of the end for traditional Indian life in Iowa.

ARTIFACTS: The Protohistoric period represents the merging of prehistory with written history. Protohistoric sites are most often marked by the presence of historic artifacts such as bottle glass and metal fragments from kettles and knives, indicating contact had been made with white explorers.

SITES IN IOWA: Protohistoric sites in Iowa you can visit include Blood Run near Rock Rapids and the Mines of Spain near Dubuque.

A.D. 1750–1950: Indians and White Settlers
Historic Period (250 to 50 years ago)

ENVIRONMENT: During the Historic period Iowa's landscape changed more than it had during any other period. Woodlands were cut down, wetlands were drained, and the prairie was torn away, all to make room for farms and towns. Buffalo, elk, wolves, passenger pigeons, and many other species disappeared from the state, and those that did not disappear greatly declined in numbers. Indians were eventually forced away or melted into the burgeoning Euroamerican population; only the Meskwaki remained as a tribe. All people steadily grew away from simple dependency on what the land freely gave and instead imposed a new design on the landscape, one that forced the land to supply their requirements.

CULTURE: Metal arrowheads and knives replaced stone tools, metal kettles replaced pottery, and firearms were traded to the tribes from the first white trading posts in Iowa. Cloth for blankets, shirts, and dresses replaced skins as tastes changed and game was depleted. Europeans and Americans built forts and other structures for military purposes and trade. Native peoples began to build cabins and frame houses in Euroamerican styles.

ARTIFACTS: The artifacts of this period are mostly the same as those found on any other historic site, with the appearance of glass, metal, and other items of European manufacture. Iowa had joined the rest of the world's economy. As far as is known, tribes had stopped making any stone tools or pottery in the Protohistoric period and became dependent on these trade goods.

SITES IN IOWA: Historic Indian sites in Iowa you can visit include the Mines of Spain near Dubuque, Iowaville near Selma, Blood Run near Rock Rapids, Wickiup Hill near Cedar Rapids, the Old Indian Agency near Keokuk, and Fort Atkinson. Some sites are on private land and require the landowner's permission to visit.

POTAWATOMI

Name means: "Keepers of the Fire," derived from Ojibwa
Other names: Pottawatomie
They call themselves: Neshnabek, "The People"
Language spoken/language family: Potawatomi/Algonkian
Residence in Iowa: 1833 to 1846
Location today: Prairie Band Potawatomi near Mayetta,
 Kansas

❨ ❨ ❨

Because many Potawatomi names are preserved in place-names of southwest Iowa, the Potawatomi are one of the better-known tribes that lived in Iowa, even though they resided in the state for only about thirteen years.

Potawatomi tradition says that the Potawatomi, the Chippewa (or Ojibwa), and the Ottawa were once one nation living on Lake Huron. The Potawatomi got their name from the Ojibwa word *potawatomink,* "Keepers of the Fire." There was a continuing association among the Potawatomi, Ottawa, and Ojibwa. The Potawatomi helped stop the Iroquois advance from the east.

By 1700 the Potawatomi had moved south and taken possession of Illinois. Some Potawatomi joined Pontiac in 1763. They moved into Indiana by 1775 after the Illinois were defeated. In 1789 the Potawatomi signed a treaty of friendship with the United States, and in 1812 they joined Tecumseh and the British. They signed a treaty in 1821 that surrendered part of southern Michigan. Their remaining Michigan lands were ceded in the Treaty of 1833 that was ratified in 1835.

After signing the Treaty of 1833, the Potawatomi moved west of the Mississippi. A band of these Potawatomi, with a small number of intermarried Ottawa and Ojibwa, settled in southwest Iowa near Council Bluffs, becoming known as the Prairie Band.

The Potawatomi agency and trading post was at Trader's Point on the Missouri River in Mills County, later renamed St. Mary's. The subagency was at Council Bluffs. One of their villages in Iowa was on the Nishnabotna River near Lewis in Cass County. Other favorite camping places were on the Nodaway River and in Coe's Grove between Stennett and Elliott.

By the provisions of the Treaty of 1846, the Prairie Band were moved from Iowa onto a reservation in Kansas, in 1846 and 1847, along with a few other families of Potawatomi, Chippewa, and Ottawa. They remained in Kansas, although for many years they returned to old sites and family graves in Iowa.

The Prairie Band of Kansas, near Holton, is the Potawatomi group associated with Iowa. Other Potawatomi groups, not connected with Iowa, are in Michigan (Hannaville Potawatomi, Huron Potawatomi, and Pokagon Potawatomi), Oklahoma (Citizen Band Potawatomi), and Wisconsin (Forest County Potawatomi).

Traditional Culture

Originally part of an ancestral Algonquian group that divided into the Potawatomi, Ojibwa, and Ottawa, the Potawatomi were known as "Keepers of the Fire." There were many different groups of Potawatomi, and their location had much influence on their way of life. Subsistence patterns were typical of Iowa's tribes since everyone depended on the same resource base. The Potawatomi were divided into patrilineal clans. The Midewiwin (or Medicine Dance) and the Drum (or Dream) Dance were two ceremonies at the heart of traditional Potawatomi religious life.

Famous Potawatomi

Spelled in different ways, Wabaunsee or Wabansi was perhaps the most famous leader of the Potawatomi during their time in Iowa.

Shabona or Shabonee, actually Ottawa by birth, is most famous for warning settlers in northern Illinois of the imminent war by Black Hawk. Ojibwa by birth, Che-Neuse or Johnny Green, leader of a small family band that lived near Marshalltown, convinced the Sioux not to attack settlers in central Iowa in 1855.

IOWAY BUFFALO HUNT

LANCE FOSTER
©1997

A CLOSER LOOK
Native Arts and Crafts

Many collectors enjoy native-made items of recent origin, either traditional material culture like wooden bowls or moccasins or contemporary expressions like paintings and jewelry.

Native art has been collected in Iowa for generations, since first contact when fur traders and the military bought clothing and curios. The Meskwaki became well known for their wooden bowls and spoons, their loom beadwork, and their handwoven yarn sashes. Since Pipestone was just over the border in Minnesota, travelers brought home to Iowa items, such as pipes and animal carvings, made from the red pipestone that has become known as catlinite. From the 1800s to the 1960s, many authentic bowls, belts, beaded items, pipes, moccasins, and other objects were readily available, as cash-poor Indian communities could earn money through these home industries. Usually, women and elders made these crafts at home, while men of working age went elsewhere for wage jobs.

With the economic changes since the 1960s, these authentic items have become increasingly rare. At the same time, interest in and demand for Indian arts have increased. As authentic native-made items are hard to find and good examples are expensive, many works of art, some promoted as being "Indian," have become available. In order for such objects to be authentic, they must be made by an Indian as defined by the Indian Arts and Crafts Act of 1990:

> The Indian Arts and Crafts Act of 1990 (P.L. 101–644) is a truth-in-advertising law that prohibits misrepresentation in marketing of Indian arts and crafts products within the United States. It is illegal to offer or display for sale, or sell any art or craft product in a manner that falsely suggests it is Indian produced, an Indian product, or the product of a particular Indian or Indian Tribe or

Indian arts and crafts organization, resident within the United States. For a first time violation of the Act, an individual can face civil or criminal penalties up to a $250,000 fine or a 5-year prison term, or both. If a business violates the Act, it can face civil penalties or can be prosecuted and fined up to $1,000,000.

Under the Act, an Indian is defined as a member of any federally or State recognized Indian Tribe, or an individual certified as an Indian artisan by an Indian Tribe.

The law covers all Indian and Indian-style traditional and contemporary arts and crafts produced after 1935. The Act broadly applies to the marketing of arts and crafts by any person in the United States. Some traditional items frequently copied by non-Indians include Indian-style jewelry, pottery, baskets, carved stone fetishes, woven rugs, kachina dolls, and clothing. . . . All products must be marketed truthfully regarding the Indian heritage and tribal affiliation of the producers, so as not to mislead the consumer. It is illegal to market an art or craft item using the name of a tribe if a member, or certified Indian artisan, of that tribe did not actually create the art or craft item.

Some of the visual artists from Iowa's historic tribes include Ruben Kent, Jean Bales, Jodi Joslin Slayton, and Patricia Joslin Smith (Ioway); Adrian Pushetonequa, Stella Young Bear, John Young Bear, Arthur Blackcloud, and Adeline Wanatee (Meskwaki); Donna Flood (Ponca); Oscar Howe (Yankton Sioux); Woody Crumbo, Mitch Battese, and Edward Mitchell (Potawatomi); and Truman Lowe, Angel DeCora, and Harry Whitehorse (Winnebago). The best resource for learning more about the traditional arts of Iowa's Meskwaki is *Art of the Red Earth People: The Mesquakie of Iowa* by Gaylord Torrence and Robert Hobbs.

If you are interested in collecting genuine Native American arts, the Indian Arts and Crafts website offers the following tips:

> When purchasing from a dealer, choose one with a good reputation.

Request a written guarantee or written verification of authenticity.

Get a receipt that includes all the vital information about your purchase, including price, maker, and maker's tribal affiliation.

Familiarize yourself with different materials and types of American Indian arts and crafts as well as the indicators of a well-made, handcrafted piece.

Realize that authentic handmade pieces may be expensive; if a price seems too good to be true, be sure to ask more questions about the item and its maker.

TRIBES OF THE ILLINOIS CONFEDERACY

Name means: Original meaning unknown, possibly "Men"
Other names: Illinois, Illini, or Illiniwek was used as the
   name for a related group of Algonquian tribes, including
   the Moingwena, Peoria, and Coiraconetanon
They call themselves: Moca (meaning unknown)
Language spoken/language family: Illinois/Algonkian
Residence in Iowa: 1667 to 1680
Location today: Peoria Tribe of Indians of Oklahoma near
   Miami, Oklahoma

☾ ☾ ☾

The Illinois lived in Iowa for only about thirteen years, but they are important in the state's history because they were the first Indians noted in Iowa by white people, the French exploration party led by Marquette down the Mississippi River in 1673. The currently accepted view is that Marquette met the Peouarea or Peoria at the mouth of the Des Moines River on the Mississippi, in northeast Missouri. While he noted on a map that the Moingwena lived to the west on the Des Moines, he did not actually visit their village. The Moingwena or Moingona gave their name to the river because of the location of their village near its mouth. Illinois groups associated with eastern Iowa during that limited period included the Coiraconetanon, Moingwena, Peoria, and Tapuaro.

Unlike many tribes, the Illinois fared well when it came to keeping their own tribal name. Because they were closely involved with the French, the French got their name right for posterity. Illini was the singular form of Illiniwek; Illini means "man" and Illiniwek means "men." The word "Illinois" is the French adaptation of Illiniwek.

The Illinois were actually not a single tribe but a loose confederacy of Algonquian-speaking tribes, including the Kaskaskia, Peoria, Michigamea, Moingwena, Cahokia, Tamaroa, Tapuaro, and Coiracoentanon (some believe the Michigamea may have originally been Siouan). The Peoria and the Tapuaro lived for a short time on the mouth of the Iowa River. The Coiracoentanon and the Moingwena lived on the Des Moines River. Originally from the Great Lakes and the Illinois area, these tribes were devastated in a series of wars with the Iroquois and others and retreated to Iowa around 1667. By the late 1670s, they had returned to Illinois and lived along both sides of the Mississippi River as far south as the mouth of the Des Moines River.

The Moingwena lived in the village of Moingona, at the mouth of the Des Moines. The Des Moines River (Rivière de Moingona) was named after this village, and later on Fort Des Moines took the name of the river. The city of Des Moines was named after the fort.

The Illinois were seriously affected by disease and by intertribal wars, especially with the Iroquois, Winnebago, Meskwaki, and Dakota. Their fortunes rose and fell with those of their French allies in the Mississippi River Valley. After successive moves to different states, including Missouri and Kansas, they were reorganized and the Peoria group took the lead. In 1868, the Peoria and other remnant Illinois groups (like the Kaskaskias), as well as some Weas and Piankashaws, were incorporated as the Confederated Peoria. Their status as a federally recognized tribe ended in 1959 as part of a federal experimental policy called termination, but their status was reinstated in 1978. Termination was intended to end the existence of Indian tribes as well as the obligations that the United States had agreed to as part of the treaty process.

Traditional Culture

Traditional Illinois culture was greatly changed early on because of their close contact with the French in the present-day state of Illinois; early French chroniclers recorded some elements. The Illinois seem to have shared the same way of life as other Central Algonquians, like the Meskwaki, and the Prairie Siouans, like the Ioway. Evidence is scarce, but there seems to have been a clan system, reported to include the Crane, Bear, Deer, and Turtle clans. Warfare with the tribes in Iowa and farther west often included raids searching for captives to sell as slaves to their French allies.

Famous Illinois

In 1769 a Peoria Indian named Black Dog was sent to assassinate Chief Pontiac, an Ottawa, and he did so by stabbing him in the back. Man-Who-Tracks was a Peoria chief depicted by the painter George Catlin in the 1830s.

"MAYANPIHI"
MAKING PEACE

LANCE FOSTER
2007

A CLOSER LOOK
Indian Houses and Landscapes

Iowa's tribes lived in large villages in the major river valleys during the warmer farming season from late spring to fall. The rivers were the major travel and trade routes, especially before the coming of the horse. Most of Iowa's tribes used dugouts rather than bark canoes.

The crop fields were located on the lower river terraces where annual flooding replenished the fertility of the soil. Corn was the staple crop, but beans, squash, pumpkins, sunflowers, melons, and tobacco were grown as well.

The summer village itself was built on the higher terraces, out of the reach of floodwaters. These larger villages were moved about every five to seven years, when soil and resources like firewood were depleted. The arrangement of the village houses may have looked somewhat haphazard to strangers, but it was based on kinship and other practical considerations. There were also special structures like drying racks for crops, sweatlodges, and small shelters to provide privacy for women during their menstrual periods.

Trails led up and out of the valleys, passing such features as areas for lacrosse games and horse racing. Finally, most graveyards and burial mounds were built on the valley rims or other high points, so as to provide an easier path to the Milky Way and the lands of the dead.

The usual type of summer house was the bark-covered lodge, oval in form, built on a gridlike frame of saplings that were tied together; other bark lodges were square. Bark houses were too leaky and drafty for winter use. People tended to live and work outside, often under the shade of an arbor attached to the front of the lodge. Smoky fires drove away insects.

The family used the indoors only for sleeping and storage and during rainy and unpleasant weather. There were benches along the walls used for sitting and sleeping, covered with finely woven bulrush mats and hides. Storage areas were under the benches, in cache pits built into the floors, and on overhead shelves. In bad weather and at night, cooking could be done indoors, but generally most cooking was done outdoors.

During the annual buffalo hunts, the people adopted the use of the tentlike buffalo-hide tipi, which was very portable. It also could withstand the fierce winds and storms of the open prairies and plains.

When the cold part of the year approached, most people left the village and split up into smaller family groups to trap beavers or hunt wildfowl, to gather sap for maple sugar, or to ice-fish. Those who were too old or ill to travel stayed behind, with family members to look after them.

These smaller winter camps were located in side valleys thick with trees and brush, which gave good protection against the winds. Also, camps were not located in the bottoms, as cold air tends to flow downslope to settle. Around the houses one could see other areas for curing hides and boiling sap.

Winter houses were much smaller, dome-shaped, and covered with tightly woven cattail mats and worn bulrush mats. Mats also covered the floors. While the bark lodges were large to accommodate extended families, the winter houses provided space only for the nuclear family; their small size, tight coverings, and small cooking fires kept them warm all winter long.

SANTEE AND YANKTON SIOUX

❨ ❨ ❨

Who are the Sioux? Early French explorers derived the name "Sioux" from the Algonquian word *nadouessioux,* meaning "snakes," because the Sioux were often enemies of Algonquian-speakers like the Ojibwa. The use of "Sioux" varies widely even among Sioux people themselves. Indeed, no term in common use collectively describes all the people of the Great Sioux Nation: Lakota, Dakota, and Nakota. Although some Indians use the word "Sioux" even today, others object to its usage as it inaccurately lumps together several independent nations and bands into one fictitious group. In olden times, each nation was referred to by the name it chose for itself, such as Sicangu or Mdewakantunwan. Whatever your view, it is best to allow the Sioux themselves to sort this out.

In prereservation days the Sioux were most strongly identified with their traditional band groups, but to some extent this has changed. Sioux reservations are scattered across the northern plains in Minnesota, North Dakota, South Dakota, Nebraska, Montana, and Canada. With the development of the reservations and the combining of several Sioux groups in some cases on a single reservation, contemporary Sioux are as likely to identify themselves by their reservation name as with their old band names.

The prehistoric Sioux homelands were in Minnesota, but groups began early on to spread west and south to hunt buffalo. The Yankton Sioux (Nakota) and Santee Sioux (Dakota) are the "Sioux" who are associated with Iowa history, primarily from 1720 to 1861. Some individuals and their families still live in Iowa today, although their tribal reservations are in other states.

The Sioux: Dakota, Nakota, and Lakota

THE EASTERN SIOUX, DAKOTA: Called Santee, from Dakota *Isanti,* a reference to an ancestral village in Minnesota near Mille Lacs, the Dakota-speaking nations were located mostly in the woodlands of Minnesota. They ranged far and wide and south into Iowa when it suited them. Four groups identified themselves as Dakota: Mdewakanton, Mdewakantunwan, "Spirit Lake Village"; Wahpeton, Wahpetunwan, "Leaf Village"; Sisseton, Sinsintunwan, "Fishysmell Village"; and Wahpekute, Wahpekute, "Shooters among the Leaves."

THE MIDDLE SIOUX, NAKOTA: Mostly found in western Minnesota, in Iowa, and into North and South Dakota, two groups spoke the Nakota form of the language: the Yankton (Ihanktunwan), "End Village," and the Yanktonais (Ihanktunwanna), "Little End Village," divided into the upper and lower Yanktonais. The Assiniboine, who also speak Nakota, left them in a dispute long ago.

THE WESTERN SIOUX, LAKOTA OR TETON SIOUX: The most famous of the Sioux, they ranged the farthest west onto the plains of North and South Dakota, Nebraska, Montana, and sometimes even farther. Unlike the Santee or Yankton, the Lakota are not associated with Iowa historically. The Lakota or Teton (from Tintatonwan, "Prairie Dwellers") were further divided into seven groups: Oglala, Sicangu, Hunkpapa, Mnikowoju, Itazipco, Oohenunpa, and Sihasapa.

Santee Sioux (Dakota)

> *Name means:* "Stone Knife People," "Allies"
> *Other names:* Eastern Sioux, Woodland Sioux
> *They call themselves:* Dakota, "Allies," or Isanti, "Stone Knife People," of which there were traditionally four groups, Wahpeton, Wahpekute, Mdewakanton, and Sisseton
> *Language spoken/language family:* Dakota/Siouan

Residence in Iowa: Prehistory to 1863

Location today: Reservations and communities in Nebraska
(Santee of Nebraska), South Dakota (Flandreau and
Crow Creek), and Minnesota (Granite Falls, Morton,
Prior Lake, and Prairie Island)

The prehistoric ancestors of the Sioux were located in upper Minnesota by about A.D. 1200. Until the 1700s, the Nakota and Dakota centered most of their early activities in Minnesota, although they sometimes hunted south into the Des Moines River headwaters or along the Big Sioux River. By the late 1700s, they were hunting more regularly along the upper Des Moines and Cedar rivers.

The two groups of Dakota who were most associated with Iowa history are the Mdewakanton and Wahpekute, whose villages were generally in Minnesota but who also hunted in northern Iowa. The Mdewakanton lived at the headwaters of the Des Moines River, in southern Minnesota. The Wahpekute controlled the headwaters of the Iowa River. The Wahpeton and Sisseton rarely came into Iowa.

In 1825, the Santee Dakota agreed to a treaty of peace with the Sauk and Meskwaki, restricting the Santee to an area mostly north of Iowa, in Minnesota, although they continued to range south for war and hunting. War over Iowa lands between the Santee and the Sauk and Meskwaki was intense and irreconcilable. The Treaty of 1825 was intended to end all Sioux occupation of Iowa.

The conflict between the Dakota and the Sauk-Meskwaki alliance was so strong that the Dakota helped the United States by fighting the Sauk in the Black Hawk War, leading to the terrible massacre of Sauk survivors, mostly women and children, who tried to flee into Iowa across the Mississippi at Bad Axe, Wisconsin.

Because of continuing friction and American expansion into Iowa, further treaties were needed to confirm the Yankton and Santee relinquishment of land claims in the state. The Yankton and Santee participated in intertribal treaties with the Sauk and Meskwaki and Ioway, ceding native lands to the United States in 1830 and 1851. The Wahpekute were especially associated with northern Iowa. The Neutral Ground was set up to protect them from the Sauk and Meskwaki to the south, but most of the Wahpekute had been wiped out by the 1850s.

In 1857, a starving band of dissident Wahpekute Dakota under Inkpaduta were angry when they found white squatters on lands they felt still belonged to the Yankton and Santee, near Okoboji Lake and Spirit Lake. They killed almost all of them in a series of attacks that became known as the Spirit Lake Massacre. They were never caught, but this conflict set the stage for the Sioux Uprising in Minnesota beginning in 1862.

Today, the Santee live on various reservations in the Dakotas, Nebraska, and Minnesota. Extensive movement and intermarriage among the Dakota and Nakota have created new communities, so that many of the Dakota of today tend to identify more with their contemporary community than with the old divisions of Wahpekute, Wahpeton, Mdewakanton, or Sisseton.

In Minnesota, the Santee Dakota live primarily at the Upper Sioux Community, Pejihutazizi, "Yellow Medicine," at Granite Falls; the Lower Sioux Community, Cansayapi, "Trees Marked Red," at Morton; the Shakopee-Mdewakanton Community, Mde Maya To, "Blue Bank Lake," at Prior Lake; and the Prairie Island Community, Tinta Wita, "Prairie Island," Mdewakanton, near Red Wing. In South Dakota, Santee live on the Crow Creek Reservation in central South Dakota, along with descendants of the Yankton. Dakota is spoken at Crow Creek. The Sisseton-Wahpeton Reservation and the Flandreau Santee Sioux (with a community, but no reservation) are also in South Dakota. In Nebraska, there are the Santee Sioux of Nebraska on the Niobrara River. Some families also live in Sioux City, Iowa.

Traditional Culture

The Santee Sioux, or Dakota proper, were essentially a woodlands group, although some bands did go onto the western prairies to join

Yankton or Lakota groups hunting buffalo. They had permanent villages of square bark lodges near rivers and lakes and grew corn, beans, squash, and pumpkins. They gathered wild rice and were successful duck hunters. They used tipis at times. They were good farmers and hunters and fished the rivers and lakes of their homelands. Many were noted as famous warriors. Like other Sioux, the Dakota did not have clans; instead, they had extended family units called *tiyospaye*. The Dakota language is very similar to the Yankton (Nakota) and Lakota languages.

Famous Santee

There were five Mdewakanton chiefs by the name of Wabasha, all in the same line, all leading the Santee through tumultuous times from before the American Revolution through the Minnesota Sioux Uprising of 1862 and 1863. Little Crow (Taoyateduta, "His Red People") was another Santee leader of outstanding ability who led and lost in the uprising. Inkpaduta ("Red Feather") was the infamous Wahpekute leader of the Spirit Lake Massacre of 1857. Charles Eastman (Ohiyesa), a Santee physician, is one of the most famous Indian authors of all time.

Yankton Sioux

> *Name means:* "End Village Allies"
> *Other names:* Yankton Sioux, Middle Sioux
> *They call themselves:* Nakota, Ihanktunwan
> *Language spoken/language family:* Nakota/Siouan
> *Residence in Iowa:* 1700 to 1853
> *Location today:* Sisseton-Wahpeton in South Dakota,
> Yankton in South Dakota

The first mention of the Yankton Sioux occurs on the map of the explorer Louis Hennepin, drawn in 1683, on which they are placed in

Minnesota north of Mille Lacs, in the region of Leech Lake or Red Lake. By 1700 they had moved westward; the French explorer Pierre-Charles Le Sueur mentions their village location near the pipestone quarry, in Minnesota. In the 1700s, they continued to live primarily in Minnesota, although they sometimes hunted down into Iowa along the headwaters of the Des Moines River or along the Big Sioux River. By 1708, Guillaume de L'Isle's map located them near the site of present-day Sioux City, in Iowa. They are next mentioned in 1804 by Lewis and Clark, as hunting the region of the James, Big and Little Sioux, Floyd, and Upper Des Moines rivers, which also included the pipestone quarry, in northwest Iowa and eastern North and South Dakota.

From 1710 to 1850, the Yankton dominated northwest Iowa from their core territory in the neighboring Dakotas. This domination may still be seen in the profusion of northwest Iowa place-names either using the word "Sioux" or bearing translations of Sioux names, such as Sioux City and the Big Sioux River. Pilot Rock, an immense granite boulder, a glacial erratic sixty feet long, forty feet wide, and about twenty feet high used as a landmark by both Indians and whites, was reported to be the reason the Sioux called the Little Sioux River the Stone River. Spirit Lake, "Lake of the Spirit Land," was the original Sioux name for both Spirit Lake and Okoboji. One legend tells that long ago people landed on an island in the lake and were instantly seized and devoured by evil spirits.

By the late 1700s, the Yankton were hunting more regularly along the Upper Des Moines and Cedar rivers. By the 1790s, they were expanding along the Upper Des Moines and were moving down along the Missouri, eastward to the Upper Iowa and even as far as Prairie du Chien. In 1804, Lewis and Clark noted the Yankton living between the Missouri and the Des Moines rivers. Lewis noted that although they were the Sioux most peacefully disposed toward whites, they would also prevent traders from ascending the Missouri past their location when they could. At that time they dressed much the same as other Sioux but had fewer guns, using mostly bows and arrows.

In 1825, the Yankton signed a peace treaty with the Sauk and Meskwaki, restricting the Yankton to an area mostly northwest of Iowa, in the Dakotas, but they continued to range south for war and hunting. Fierce fighting over Iowa lands between the Yankton and the Sauk, Meskwaki, and Ioway continued.

By the 1840s the Yankton had centered their activities along the Vermillion River in South Dakota. Because of continuing friction and American expansion into Iowa, further treaties were needed to confirm the Yankton and Santee relinquishment of land claims in Iowa. The Yankton and Santee participated in intertribal treaties with the Sauk and Meskwaki and Ioway, ceding native lands to the United States in 1830 and 1851; in 1830, the Yankton ceded 2.2 million acres.

The Treaty of 1858 caused the Yankton to cede lands that included more than eleven million acres in South Dakota, leaving a reservation of 430,00 acres near Fort Randall. They retained a claim on the 648.2-acre Pipestone Reservation until 1929, then sold it on the condition of federal assurance of access to the pipestone quarries. When the Dakota began the 1862 Sioux Uprising, Yankton Chief Palaneapape kept the Yankton from joining.

Following the General Allotment Act of 1887, the Yankton reservation was divided and allotted by 1890. The Yankton were subsequently scattered across many reservations.

The Yankton Sioux can be found, among other places, on the Sisseton Reservation, the Crow Creek Reservation, and the Yankton Sioux Reservation as well as at Standing Rock and Rosebud, all in South Dakota. Some also live on the Fort Peck Reservation in Montana. Individual families also live in Iowa, in Sioux City, Des Moines, and Ames.

Traditional Culture

The Yankton were a true Plains people, living in tipis like the Lakota. They were buffalo hunters and ranged far onto the plains on horseback in their communal hunts, along with their Yanktonais and

Lakota relatives. Like the other Sioux groups, the Yankton did not have clans but were organized into many *tiyospaye* or extended family bands.

Although other tribes like the Ioway and Otoe had originally used the pipestone quarry of Minnesota, by 1700 the Yankton had asserted control and served as intermediaries to other tribes seeking stone for their pipes. Today several Yankton families are recognized pipemakers and still have the traditional rights to quarry stone there.

Famous Yankton

Wanata ("The Charger") was a Yankton chief who fought the Americans until the War of 1812, when he befriended them. He was especially noted for organizing warfare against the Ojibwa and Ioway. War Eagle was actually Santee by birth but moved west and was elected a chief by the Yankton; his grave and memorial are near Sioux City. Palaneapape ("Struck-by-the-Ree") sent a warning to whites in Dakota during the Minnesota Sioux Uprising of 1862, saving hundreds of American lives. As a baby, he was wrapped in an American flag by Lewis and Clark, who proclaimed that he would grow up to be a great leader; Struck-by-the-Ree would lead the Yankton into the 1880s. The Deloria family has contributed many distinguished educators and scholars, including anthropologist Ella Deloria and probably the most famous Indian author of all time, Vine Deloria, Jr. Other noted and respected Yankton include Leonard Brughier, educator, and Maria Pearson, an activist for native rights and an advocate for burial protection laws.

The Spirit Lake Massacre

Inkpaduta (1815–1882), a Wahpekute Santee Sioux, was the leader of the renegade band of about fifteen individuals involved in the Spirit Lake Massacre of 1857. He became the leader when his father, Wamdesapa, died in 1848. This small band was a disaffected group of tribal outlaws and castoffs from different Santee groups that the rest of the Wahpekute had rejected. Inkpaduta's hatred of whites apparently began when his brother and his brother's family were murdered by the white outlaw Henry Lott. After that, Inkpaduta resisted any white encroachment on lands in Iowa, Minnesota, and South Dakota, although he also demanded annuity payments from treaties that the Wahpekute majority had signed.

The winter of 1856–57 was very severe, and both whites and Indians suffered. Most of the Santee had signed the Treaty of 1851 and thus received a bare living from annuities. Inkpaduta's band did not receive annuities, so they survived by begging and stealing from white settlements. When one of their band was bitten by a settler's dog, they shot it. An angry white posse surrounded them and forced them to give up their weapons. Unable to hunt, Inkpaduta's men somehow regained weapons and went on a two-day spree, killing settlers near Spirit Lake on March 8 and 9, 1857. They killed thirty-five settlers and captured four women. Two of the women died; the other two, Margaret Marble and Abbie Gardner, were ransomed by other Santee and returned to the whites.

In 1862, during the Minnesota Uprising of several Santee groups, Inkpaduta helped achieve victory at the battles of Bog Mound and White Stone Hill. The Santee in general took the blame again for the actions of Inkpaduta and his band. Although the uprising was finally put down by U.S. troops, Inkpaduta himself was not captured.

Inkpaduta next appeared as one of the few Santee who fought

Custer, along with Lakota like Crazy Horse and Sitting Bull, at the Little Bighorn in 1876. After the Lakota were defeated, Inkpaduta fled north into Canada, never making peace with the whites. Some say he died there, while others say he died on the Fort Peck Reservation in Montana in 1882.

WINNEBAGO

Name means: "Stinking Water," derived from Algonquian
winnepeko, referring to Green Bay, Wisconsin
Other names: Hochunk
They call themselves: Hochunkara, Hochunk, Hocak,
Hochugara, etc., translated variously as "The People of
the Big (Original) Voice," indicating that Hochunk was
the original language
Language spoken/language family: Hochunk/Siouan
Residence in Iowa: 1832 to 1846, although some families
stayed after removal in 1846
Location today: Winnebago Tribe of Nebraska near Macy,
Nebraska; Ho-Chunk Nation near Black River Falls,
Wisconsin

❨ ❨ ❨

"Winnebago" was the name given to this tribe by Algonquian-
speaking tribes, neighbors of the Winnebago, who lived near Green
Bay, Wisconsin. Winnebago, from *winnepeko,* means something like
"Stinking Water," referring to the fishy-smelling shores of Green Bay
on Lake Michigan.

The "Winnebago" actually called themselves Hochunkara, which
meant something like the "People of the Great Language" or "People
of the Big Voice," "big" meaning originating in earliest times. Some
Ioway and Otoe traditions point to the Hochunkara as that portion
of the original people who stayed near the Great Lakes when clans
who would become the Ioway and Otoe decided to move away in
search of new lands on the prairies.

Today, some branches of the Hochunkara have decided to re-
ject the foreign term "Winnebago" in favor of variations from their

own language, Hochunk. In Wisconsin, they are known as the Ho-Chunk; in Nebraska, they are the Winnebago.

The Winnebago's earliest known residence was at a place they called Red Banks, near Green Bay, on Lake Michigan in Wisconsin. Their traditions maintained that this was their place of origin and that other tribes such as the Ioway, Otoe, and Missouri split off from them. The Ioway and Otoe language developed from the same ancestral language which gave rise to Hochunkara as it is known today. Finally, archaeological evidence indicates both a common origin for these cultures, centered in Wisconsin, and considerable interaction and population movement in the region.

The Winnebago first traded with the French, but when England took Canada they became British allies and joined Tecumseh against the Americans in the War of 1812. They remained in their Wisconsin homelands. In 1827 they began to resist American incursions into their territory in Wisconsin and Illinois, a situation sometimes called the Winnebago War, and American troops from St. Louis were sent to prevent outright war. On August 11, 1827, they signed a friendship treaty with the United States under their chief Huchup. Continuing American invasions of their lands, especially in search of lead deposits, brought more conflicts. A treaty providing for boundaries and compensation was signed at Green Bay in 1828. The very next year, they ceded a tract south of the Wisconsin River.

The involvement of a few Winnebago, such as Winneshiek, in the Black Hawk War of 1832 was used by the United States as a pretext to force them into more cessions. As partial payment for Wisconsin and Illinois lands ceded to the United States in the Treaty of 1832, the Winnebago were assigned lands in northeast Iowa on the Turkey River, in an area called the Neutral Ground.

In 1839, a Winnebago group went to Iowa to scout for village locations, provoking Keokuk to demand that they should be sent south of the Missouri River instead. The Winnebago were pleased neither with the Neutral Ground nor with Keokuk's demand. They wanted to remain in their Wisconsin homelands. In 1840, they met at Prairie du Chien to try to convince the Americans to let them remain in Wisconsin. The American authorities refused and further stated that the 1841 annuity payments would be made only at the Neutral Ground Agency. The Winnebago reluctantly and in small groups made the move. For a long time they simply lingered on the edge of the danger zone, on the western bank of the Mississippi. Retreat was impossible, as the U.S. Army had burned and destroyed their canoes to prevent their return to Wisconsin.

The Neutral Ground was not neutral at all. Originally established to separate the Sioux to the north and the Sac and Meskwaki to the south, through the terms of the Treaty of 1825, the Neutral Ground had become unclaimed land marked by incessant warring between the Sioux and the Sauk and Meskwaki. The Winnebago were stuck in a dangerous spot between two old enemies; they were raided from both sides, and some were killed.

Fort Atkinson was built by the U.S. Army as a protective measure, but it was considered a failure in the effort to ensure intertribal peace. As a result, the Winnebago were moved out of Iowa by 1846, when they ceded the Neutral Ground to the United States and moved to a tract north of the St. Peter's River on the Upper Mississippi. Finally, they were assigned a reservation in Nebraska, where they live today. Others quietly returned to ancestral lands in Wisconsin.

As a tribe, the Winnebago had actually lived in Iowa's Neutral Ground only from 1841 to 1846. However, for years afterward, they returned to favorite spots in Iowa for trapping and hunting. Some families continued to do this into the 1900s.

Traditional Culture

The Winnebago are part of the Woodland culture group. They were the most powerful nation of the western Great Lakes in prehistoric times, but a series of wars and epidemics in the protohistoric period almost destroyed them. Their social organization was built around a complex clan bundle system as well as religious societies such as the Medicine Dance. Many Winnebago still follow traditional religious and clan ways, especially in Wisconsin.

Famous Winnebago

Among famous Winnebago have been Waukon, Waukon Decorah, Nawkaw, Hoowanneka, Winneshiek, Reuben Snake, Mountain Wolf Woman, and Emma Big Bear. The first five were chiefs during the wars and removal period. Reuben Snake was a contemporary leader who claimed Iowa symbolically for the Winnebago. Mountain Wolf Woman described the old ways in her notable autobiography. Emma Big Bear was the last Winnebago to live the traditional life in Iowa; she died in 1968.

IOWAY FALL POWWOW

LANCE FOSTER
© 1997

A CLOSER LOOK
Going to a Powwow

Going to a powwow is the best introduction for most people who want to learn more about Indian culture. There are different styles of dancing, regalia, crafts to buy, goods to try like frybread or Indian tacos, and interesting people to meet. Common steps you may see, with their associated dancer regalia, include straight dance, fancy dance, grass dance, jingle dress, and gourd dance.

The most popular powwows in Iowa include one at the Meskwaki Settlement in summer and two at Iowa State University and the University of Iowa in the spring. At times other powwows may be held around Iowa. There are also excellent powwows in surrounding states, such as at the Omaha Reservation in Nebraska. Schedules and details can change, so it is best to contact the sources directly for details.

Behavior at a powwow calls for respectful common sense. Stand when everyone stands, and sit when everyone sits. Don't take pictures when the announcer says not to, and ask for permission before you take photos of anyone. Walk around the edge of the dance arena if you have to; never walk across it. If you are invited to eat by Indian friends, it is good manners to accept, and eat whatever you are offered. Do not go out and dance unless the master of ceremonies makes a loudspeaker announcement calling for participation by all.

VISITING NATIONS

❨ ❨ ❨

Other tribes may have entered Iowa at one time or another, but they were not true residents of Iowa. Their historical significance is attached to homelands in other states. Some sought a temporary refuge, some came to fight and to raid the tribes that lived here, some came to hunt, and some visited resident tribes for short or extended periods.

Most stayed for only a year or two or for a few weeks now and again, and we know of many of these visits only because of French historians and mapmakers as well as tribal traditions. The visitors of historic record included the Ottawa and Huron, the Miami and Wea, Kickapoo, Mascouten, and Chippewa or Ojibwa, all of whom came from the north and east for a year or two. Others are known through traditional native stories of Comanche, Padouca, Osage, and Kansa raids from the south and west.

Kansa and Osage, Late 1700s to Early 1800s

The Siouan-speaking Osage and Kansa were related to the Omaha and Ponca. The Osage lived in Missouri and Oklahoma, while the Kansa or Kaw lived in Kansas. Both the Osage and the Kansa were generally at war with the Sauk and Meskwaki and often the Ioway, who were all expanding south and west into the Osage and Kansa territories in Missouri and Kansas. In the late 1700s and early 1800s, the Osage and Kansa would occasionally hunt and raid into Iowa.

Kickapoo, 1728

The Kickapoo were Algonquian-speaking Woodland nations that on occasion wandered into Iowa to hunt or make war. Historic records mention one camp in 1728. Like other tribes, most of the Kickapoo were removed to Kansas and Oklahoma. A very traditional group of Kickapoo live on the border of Texas and Mexico, with others living farther into Mexico.

Lenni Lenape or Delaware, 1833–1846

The Lenni Lenape or Delaware were great travelers from time immemorial according to their sacred tradition, known as the Walum Olum, and generally were respected by many tribes. For a time a few Lenape families lived with the Potawatomi in Iowa, before they were moved to new homes in Kansas, then Oklahoma, where their descendants live today. There was also a battle between a small hunting band of Lenni Lenape and Sioux near West Des Moines.

Mascouten, Late 1600s to 1700s

The Mascouten were an eastern Algonquian tribe which made raids for slaves into Iowa in the late 1600s from their homelands across the Mississippi. They were part of the movement of eastern tribes like the Miami, Wea, and Kickapoo into Iowa as a result of the Iroquois wars to the east.

In the late 1600s, the Mascouten were allied with the Meskwaki and in conflict with the French. They also fought the Ioway and the Sioux. Because of fierce French pressure on the Meskwaki, the Mascouten and Kickapoo abandoned the Meskwaki cause in 1728. They even joined the French and Illinois attacks on the Meskwaki in 1730 and 1731. The Mascouten eventually allied with the Kickapoo, Potawatomi, and others, but though they were loyal to the French and then the British, they refused to fight the Americans. In 1788 they were still a separate group, but by 1813 they had become incorporated into the Kickapoo. Today they no longer exist as a separate group. What little is known of Mascouten culture indicates an organi-

zation into clans; their culture seems to have been similar to that
of other central Algonquians like the Kickapoo and Meskwaki. The
name Muscatine, which is usually translated as "prairie," may be a
surviving memory of this tribe.

Miami and Wea and Piankashaw, 1670s

The Miami were an association of Algonquian tribes centered farther east in Indiana, although their forays took them into Illinois and
Wisconsin and, briefly, into Iowa for a few years in the 1670s. They
were often allies of the Mascouten and the Kickapoo. Although at
first they were all called Miami, the Wea and Piankashaw later at-
tained independent status. They were at war with the Dakota and Ioway and would sometimes make raids into Iowa from Illinois. Today,
their descendants live in Oklahoma as the Confederated Peoria.

Ojibwa or Chippewa, 1784

The Ojibwa or Chippewa homelands were farther north, in Minnesota, Michigan, and Canada. There was one Ojibwa camp in Iowa in
1784. A few Ojibwa families also joined with the Potawatomi during
their time in Iowa. Ojibwa bands probably entered northeast Iowa
along the Mississippi during hunting or raiding. The Ojibwa, Potawatomi, and Ottawa were historical allies.

Ottawa and Huron, 1657–1660

From 1657 to 1660, a small band of Iroquoian-speaking Huron and
Ottawa (actually two separate tribes) fled from their homelands to
Iowa because of the Iroquois war to the east, but they soon returned
due to their dislike for the prairie country and conflict with the Dakota. A few Ottawa families are said to have lived among the Potawatomi during their time in Iowa.

Padouca (Plains Apache and Comanche), 1600s–1800s

Some Ioway and Otoe stories speak of swift raids from the southwest, mostly in Nebraska but occasionally into Iowa, by the Comanche, also known as the Padouca or Ietan by the Siouans and French in the 1700s. In the 1500s and 1600s, the name Padouca was applied to the Plains Apache, including the Kiowa-Apache and Lipan Apache. The Padouca lived in western Kansas, western Nebraska, and Colorado. These horsemen came to the Missouri River village tribes, including the Pawnee, from the 1600s to the 1800s to raid for slaves to be sold to buyers in what is now New Mexico. Peace was made between the Padouca and the Missouri River tribes through efforts by the French trader Etienne de Bourgmont in 1724.

DOCTORING   WASWEHI   LANCE FOSTER ©2005

A CLOSER LOOK
Do You Have Indian Blood?

Native American heritage forms part of every American's identity in some way, historical, ancestral, and cultural, whether you actually have native blood or not. The encounter between the western and eastern hemispheres, for better or worse, made us what we are today. Many families tell stories about ancestors being "part Indian." Some know the names of these ancestors, while others don't have much more than vague rumors to go on.

As settlement continued west, some white settlers occasionally married or had relations with Indians, most often a white man with an Indian woman. Over many generations, the exact history of the family would be lost, often out of shame and prejudice. This is a sad fact, and as a rule little can be done to recover these family histories. Whenever possible, most families who were lighter-skinned married among white people and tried to pass as white themselves. Darker relatives tended to marry other darker mixed-bloods or Indians, and so families often drifted apart.

Although today some people hope to reclaim their connection with half-remembered Indian ancestors, usually through genealogical studies, success at such studies can be difficult to achieve. These people will often have to be content with family stories and proud of the connections that those stories pass down.

Three kinds of people generally try to connect with their Native American past.

People who have heard family stories that they had an Indian ancestor or "have some Indian blood." The family is vague about the details or says the ancestor was part Cherokee or Blackfeet, but no one really is sure who it was or how far back it was. These people have a difficult road to travel. There's no way they can go further in their quest until they answer some basic genealogical questions about their family. It takes work and a good chunk of time, dedication, and faith. More and more is available on the Internet. Look at the resource links to find out how to get started. Every U.S. census has different categories, and some include native status. Although it is reported that DNA tests may indicate a connection to biological native ancestry, these tests cannot determine tribal identity, which is political rather than biological.

People who have studied their family genealogy and have a good idea which ancestor is Indian but have trouble finding out which tribe that ancestor might belong to. There is no systematic information online (or anywhere else) that tells which family names are definitively associated with which tribe. One way this can be done is through checking family names against tribal rolls, usually from the 1880s during the time when Indians were determining tribal membership for the Dawes Allotment Act. The Dawes Act aimed at dividing up lands held in common as tribal lands, which would make Indians assimilate into white society and would open up more lands to non-Indians. Each tribal member would be assigned a block of acreage, and the remainder would be sold to white settlers. Some tribes do have earlier rolls, for instance the Cherokees in the eastern United States, but for most tribes, including those of Iowa, anything earlier than 1880 or so is generally too early for specific surnames. The reality is that checking tribal rolls is useful only for people who know the names of Indian ancestors who lived between 1880 and 1920. To get a look at tribal rolls, you need to contact the appropriate tribes; resources for a particular tribe may also be online.

People who are Native American but were adopted by non-Indian families and have lost connection with their tribe or don't know what tribe they came from, as well as people who are descendants of this group. It may be tough if not impossible to get to your adoption records, but that is the place to start. If you learn who your birth parents are, it can be as simple as reestablishing contact with relatives on the reservation. Someone may actually have been looking for you for a long time. Without knowing to whom you are related, it will be impossible to go any further. The same goes for the children and grandchildren of the original adoptees. This can be frustrating, especially for people who "look Indian" but don't know anything about "being Indian." Some groups are beginning to try to make connections between these "lost children" and the tribes they came from; one of these is the Lost Bird Society. If an adoptee cannot make the connection, he or she needs to make a choice: go on living as a non-Indian, or try to form new connections and friendships with nearby tribes or urban Indian communities.

The first step, one absolutely required for discovering your family's past, is to research your family genealogy. You have to do this yourself, unless you decide to pay a professional genealogical researcher. Much information is available on the Internet. Genealogy is a complicated and lengthy process, often requiring years of archival work to find a single name or date. You may be lucky enough to find what you are looking for in just one step. Or you may find that a distant relative has done much of the work already. But genealogy is much like hunting for gold: you need to know what you are doing and look in the right places, but often luck seems to be just as important. For genealogical resources, see the information at the end of the book.

A NEW PEOPLE: THE MIXED-BLOODS

❨ ❨ ❨

A new people were born from the mixing of whites (usually French) and Indians. These people were historically called mixed-bloods or "half-breeds," the latter now considered a derogatory term. Another term is the French "Métis," which means "mixed," most often applied to the French-Indian population of Canada and the Upper Missouri country. The Métis served as interpreters in the fur trade and were looked to for aid by both whites and Indians, although they were also often looked upon with suspicion by both whites and Indians.

The earliest mixed-bloods were born of the marriages and liaisons of French fur-trader fathers and Indian mothers, often arranged for the purpose of trading alliances. Many of the earliest "white" settlements were really founded by mixed-bloods who settled at trading sites, such as those that became Prairie du Chien, Wisconsin; St. Joseph, Missouri; St. Louis, Missouri; Council Bluffs, Iowa; Sioux City, Iowa; and Davenport, Iowa. Some of their children rose to prominence in frontier society.

Louis Tesson, the first "white" farmer in Iowa, was actually a mixed-blood. Antoine Le Claire, one of the founders of Davenport, was the son of a Potawatomi woman and a French father and married a Sauk woman. He worked for the federal government and interpreted for the Black Hawk Treaty of 1832; as a result, his wife was granted land by the Sauk and Meskwaki. He also interpreted for several other treaties, such as the 1842 Sac and Fox Treaty.

The Sauk and Meskwaki relinquished title to all lands in Missouri in the Treaty of 1824. Under one of the terms of that treaty, a portion of southeast Iowa was set aside for the occupation of "half-breed" "Sac and Foxes." This tract, which became known as the Half-Breed Tract or Half-Breed Reservation, consisted of 119,000 acres between the Mississippi and Des Moines rivers in present-day Lee County, Iowa. Most of the land recipients were Sauk mixed-bloods. In 1834, the government allowed the "half-breed" landowners to sell their property and move west, which most apparently did. Almost all settlers who lived on the Half-Breed Tract in Iowa after 1835 were white settlers who bought out the mixed-blood parcels and who did not have any Sauk blood.

The provisions of the Treaty of 1830 marked out a similar tract on Otoe lands in Nebraska. That tract, bordering the Missouri River between the Great Nemaha River and the Little Nemaha, was set aside by the Otoe, with payments by the Ioway, Omaha, and Yankton for the mixed-blood children of those tribes (including the Otoe). The tract was known as the Great Nemaha Reservation (after the river) or Half-Breed Tract. That reservation was also allotted to individual owners in 1860 and was eventually bought out by white settlers. The Great Nemaha Reservation should not be confused with the present Iowa Reservation, farther south adjacent to Whitecloud, Kansas, which is bordered on the north by the Little Nemaha River.

A CLOSER LOOK
Indians in Iowa Today

Today, Indian people face a very different Iowa than they did in the past and the same daily challenges that everyone else does. However, as Indians, they face additional obstacles and issues.

Indian Communities in Iowa

The 1995 Statistical Profile of Iowa, from the Public Interest Institute, Iowa Department of Economic Development, states that in 1980 there were 5,455 Native Americans in Iowa, less than 1 percent, or about 0.19 percent of Iowa's total population. In 1990, the figure rose to 7,349 Native Americans in Iowa, still less than 1 percent, at about 0.26 percent. In 2000, according to the U.S. Census Bureau, there were 8,989 Native Americans in Iowa, out of 2,929,324 people, less than one-third of 1 percent, or 0.3 percent; by 2008, that figure had risen to 0.4 percent. This trend may represent a rise in the native population, or it may simply indicate that more people are claiming Indian blood as part of the census option to self-identify as Indian.

There are three tribal groups with trust lands in Iowa, the Meskwaki, the Omaha, and the Winnebago. The 2000 census lists 761 residents on Meskwaki lands; 632 of those were Indian. No residents were listed for the Omaha or Winnebago lands in Iowa. Only a few acres each, these lands are occupied by casinos.

Native Americans today do not have to live on Indian reservations. Like any other American they have the right to live wherever they like. In fact, there was a formalized U.S. government policy in the 1950s and 1960s to relocate many Indian people to urban areas where there were supposed to be more job and educational opportunities.

Many historical factors like relocation, job availability, marriage outside the tribe, education, land loss, or a desire to see new places have resulted in Indian people residing all over Iowa and the United States, not necessarily in their ancient homelands. Only the Meskwaki still have land in Iowa which they own and on which they reside as a distinct community. The Omaha and the Winnebago have small tracts of land on which they, like the Meskwaki, have built tribal casinos, which help fund tribal programs. And in several of Iowa's cities, there are neighborhoods to which Indians are attracted because there are jobs and relatives there.

The most notable of these cities is Sioux City, which draws many Indians because of its proximity to the Yankton, Santee, Winnebago, and Omaha reservations on the other side of the Missouri River. Other large cities like Des Moines and Davenport attract Indians because of economic opportunities. Cities with colleges and universities, like Iowa City and Ames, often have notable Indian populations, as Indian students not only attend programs there but also stay and raise families. Even in smaller towns and rural areas Indians are occasionally found, due to intermarriage or adoption or because they are near tribal lands, like Tama and Toledo.

Tribes historically located in or near Iowa continue to be the majority, especially if they have lands in Iowa or nearby states, like the Meskwaki (Iowa), Dakota (Minnesota, Nebraska, the Dakotas), Winnebago (Nebraska), and Omaha (Nebraska). But it is also not uncommon to find tribes from far away, like Navajo (from the Southwest) or Cherokee (from Oklahoma or North Carolina), because of better educational and job opportunities in Iowa.

Indian Education and Programs

Some of Iowa's community colleges, colleges, and universities have courses about Indians. At least three have departments or interdisciplinary programs focused specifically on Indian studies. Programs often change, so contact those you are interested in for the latest information.

In 1973, Morningside College in Sioux City started an Indian studies program that had excellent connections to the nearby Winnebago and Omaha reservations as well as an active Indian student organization, the Red Road Council. Iowa State University offers a minor through its American Indian Studies Program. ISU also has the United Native American Student Association and has sponsored the annual Symposium on the American Indian, with a powwow and noted native guests, for more than twenty-five years. The University of Iowa has an American Indian and Native Studies Program, which grants an undergraduate minor as well as undergraduate and graduate certificates. It is especially noted for its program in Native American law, and it has several native student organizations such as the American Indian Student Association, which organizes the University of Iowa's annual powwow and a two-week Iowa First Nations Summer Program for students entering eighth or ninth grade. The University of Northern Iowa has a Native American Student Union.

All of Iowa's public institutions participate in the Iowa First Nations program, which grants in-state tuition status to members of Indian nations historically connected to Iowa. These tribes currently include Ioway, Kickapoo, Menominee, Miami, Ojibwa/Chippewa, Omaha, Otoe, Ottawa/Odawa, Potawatomi, Sac and Fox/Sauk/Meskwaki, Sioux, and Winnebago. The criteria by which these tribes were selected are unclear, for while certain of the listed tribes are well established in their connection to Iowa (Omaha, Yankton, Meskwaki, Ioway, Sauk, some of the Santee bands, Potawatomi, Otoe, and Winnebago), others were not true residents of Iowa or entered only briefly to raid or visit resident tribes (for example, Ojibwa, Huron, Ottawa, Menominee, and Miami). A small band of Ottawa were in Iowa for only three years, from 1657 to 1660, with a small group of Huron; why the Ottawa are included and the Huron are not is a mystery. Still other tribes that could lay potentially valid claims to being resident are not included on the list.

There are also urban Indian programs that center on job training and health, as well as elementary and secondary education. Many of these are based in Sioux City and serve economically disadvantaged Indian families; the Circle of First Nations of Central Iowa is in Des Moines. On May 12, 2008, Governor Chet Culver signed legislation creating the Iowa Commission on Native American Affairs, housed in the Department of Human Rights.

Alcohol treatment programs focus on the special problems faced by Indian communities, through culturally appropriate approaches using sweatlodges and other traditional ways. Most of these are non-profit programs dependent on grants, so lack of funding can cause otherwise successful programs to shut down.

Contemporary Issues

Indian people continue to fight for their cultural existence and sovereignty, the right to self-rule and self-determination. Following are some of the contemporary issues that affect Native Americans in Iowa.

Native people suffer a higher than average rate of diabetes. This is a result in large part of the poor diet associated with a higher poverty rate. Many native communities suffer from substance abuse of both alcohol and drugs. Again, much of the blame can be attributed to the high rate of poverty and social stress, although there are indications that genetic factors may also contribute to alcoholism.

Iowa is racially homogenous, and while mostly white, it is a fairly tolerant state. However, racially motivated incidents continue to mar the state's reputation, usually in areas with large Indian populations. For decades near the Meskwaki Settlement, for example, Indians were shot and killed or beaten up and laid on a lonely stretch of railroad track to be crushed by an oncoming train.

Sioux City has a relatively large Indian population from tribes with reservations in Nebraska and South Dakota. Discrimination in jobs, housing, and other arenas continues to this day, though there have been attempts to address the situation, and state and federal laws such as the Iowa Civil Rights Act and the Fair Housing Act prohibit such discrimination. The Iowa Department of Human Services, for example, is working to address the "disproportionate number of Native American children involved in the child welfare system" in Woodbury County.

As long as people see another group of people as different, somehow "less," it is easy to drift into racism and violence. Even those who idealize Indians as somehow nobler or more spiritual are stereotyping. Indians are people, no better or worse, with the same good and bad points as individuals in any other group.

A slippery slope faced by many Indians is that requirements for tribal enrollment may result in a loss of connections to their tribe. Ask a hundred people what it means to be "Indian," and you will get a hundred different answers. Certainly the recognition of an individual as a member by his or her tribe is of singular importance. Every tribe has the right to set its own standards for enrollment, that is, for what legally constitutes membership in the enrolling tribe. All tribes base enrollment upon ancestors having been enrolled in the tribe on an original census roll. Some tribes are very strict, demanding not only a high percentage of blood but even either patrilineal (through the father) or matrilineal (through the mother) descent. Others require only descent from an enrolled member; this can mean minimal Indian blood for some. Also, it is a general rule that a person can be enrolled in only one tribe, so that someone who is half Navajo and half Sioux has to pick one or the other and thus may be considered only half Indian. And of course Indian children adopted by white parents have often lost their tribal connections forever.

Today it is not always easy to determine who is Indian simply by appearance. Some "look Indian" but may not be; on the other hand, some who are blond and blue-eyed may be enrolled in a tribe.

At one time it was very hard and sometimes dangerous to be Indian, given the prejudice and poverty that were faced every day. But as movies like *Dances with Wolves* made being Indian seem romantic and spiritual, and as tribal casinos became profitable, suddenly there were hordes of self-described Indians who were very interested in finding their roots—and a share in casino profits or scholarships. There are also many non-Indian hobbyists who dress up and enjoy "playing Indian," even taking Indian-sounding names. Some Indians call these people Wannabees or Pretendians.

Even whether to use the term "Indian" or "Native American" can result in disagreement. Indian people have on occasion used the term "Indian," only to be corrected by a white person who believes "Native American" to be more sensitive. Currently, either term is fine, though most Indians use "Indian." Other terms used over the years include "First Nations," "Indigenous People," "Amerind," "Amerindian," and "Native Peoples," but it is best usually to refer to people by their tribal affiliation.

Traditionally the poorest racial group in America, Indians have come upon the bonanza of gaming. Most started with small bingo operations and negotiated their way through gaming compacts with a state government, ending up with full-fledged casinos. For many tribes, this has been an economic windfall, providing funds for infrastructure, health, and education. In some instances but not all, annuity payments are made to individual tribal members.

Not all tribes have casinos, and, of those that do, not all provide money to tribal members. There are often allegations of corruption as part of tribal politics. Non-Indians are often jealous of a tribe's apparent financial success. There are also some anti-gambling movements that are really anti-Indian movements. However, the casinos employ many local non-Indians and provide financial gain to the non-Indian businesses and communities that service the casino and its customers. One issue brought up in the Indian community is the negative effect casinos may have on local family and traditional life, such as through the continuing loss of language use and incidents of strife among tribal members. In any case, as long as the casino phenomenon continues, Indian communities that have them will be able to be more economically self-sufficient.

Many Indians have taken up the issue of the use of Indian mascots by sports teams. Using racist terms like "Redskins" or having fake "Indian chiefs" doing a goofy "woo-woo" dance while shaking a tomahawk further strengthens the stereotyping of Indians and their traditions, reducing them to cartoonish figures and dehumanizing them. In 2007 the University of Illinois Board of Trustees retired Chief Illiwinek, mascot of the University of Illinois at Urbana-Champaign, but retained the nickname Fighting Illini. However, some students want to reinstate the mascot despite protests from the university's Native American House and American Indian Studies faculty.

Racism's more harmful effects, such as hate crimes, require the reduction of a group of people to a stereotype. Even if you don't always understand why people are hurt by something, it's all about treating people with respect, something we all want.

Final Words

Iowa is rich with the history and culture of its native nations, with sites and memories of the past and with the ongoing changes of a living people who will not be bound by the definitions of others. With this book, you have been introduced to an outline . . . an outline that you need to fill in personally, through your own travels to Iowa's ancient places and through your own experiences of the contemporary community of its American Indian peoples and events. Reading this book was simply one step in your own journey of connecting with the land and the Indians of Iowa.

There is much to learn from the First People of the Americas if we all are to survive the challenges of modern life. Iowa's history shows that its Native Americans have survived extreme times before. "This

Land between Two Rivers," Iowa itself, is a keeper of continuity and hope. To paraphrase an old saying I have heard from the Meskwaki, who found in Iowa their final refuge:

The East is too bloody,
The South is too hot,
The West is too dry,
The North is too cold,
Here, it is just right.

PLACES TO VISIT

Iowa has dozens of sites associated with Native American history that the interested public can visit, from archaeological and historic sites to museums and casinos. The following is a list of some of the best-known, alphabetized by city or town. Addresses are accurate as of May 2009. In addition, the National Archives, Central Plains Region, http://www.archives.gov/central-plains/kansas-city, serving Iowa, Kansas, Missouri, and Nebraska, contains extensive records and exhibits and provides tours.

Ackworth

Woodland Mounds Preserve. http://www.warrenccb.org/areas/areas .html. From Ackworth (east of Indianola) go south about 1 mile on County S23, then turn east and go about 2.5 miles. Several Woodland mounds are located in the preserve.

Agency

Grave of Chief Wapello. http://www.desmoinesriver.org/chief_wapello _memorial_in_agency.htm. Buried beside friend General Joseph Street, agent to Sac and Fox.

Ames

Iowa State University. http://www.iastate.edu. Archaeology and Indian artifact exhibits in the Anthropology Department, Curtis Hall. The annual Symposium on the American Indian is held each spring along with the powwow.

Boone

Boone County Cultural Center and Historical Museum. 602 Story Street. Exhibits include Indian artifacts.

Boone County Museum. 1004 Story Street. Includes an American Indian display.

Ledges State Park. http://www.iowadnr.com/parks/state_park_list/ledges.html. Long inhabited by Native Americans, Ledges has numerous archaeological sites, including mounds; it was also a favored meeting place for Sioux, Meskwaki, and Sauk.

Cedar Falls

University of Northern Iowa Museum. http://www.uni.edu/museum. Collection includes ethnological pieces from the Americas.

Cedar Rapids

The History Center, Linn County Historical Society. http://www.historycenter.org. Collections include Indian artifacts and an exhibit on Iowa archaeology.

Wickiup Hill Outdoor Learning Center. http://www.mycounty parks.com/County/Linn/Park/Wickiup-Hill-Outdoor-Learning-Center.aspx. On the site of a historic Meskwaki village, this new center has exhibits on both prehistoric and historic native people.

Cherokee

Pilot Rock. Three miles south of Cherokee on Highway 59 on Pilot Rock Road. The red quartzite glacial erratic (14 feet high, 180 feet in circumference) was used as a landmark by Indians and, later, whites.

Sanford Museum and Planetarium. http://sanfordmuseum.org. Exhibits on Pleistocene megafauna, Archaic and Woodland periods, Great Oasis, Mill Creek, and Oneota.

Corydon

Prairie Trails Museum of Wayne County. http://www.prairietrails museum.org. Collections include Native American artifacts.

Council Bluffs

Lewis and Clark Monument and Scenic Overlook, Lewis and Clark State Park. www.iowadnr.com/parks/state_park_list/lewis_clark .html. Commemorates the meeting of Lewis and Clark with Otoe and Missouria Indians on August 3, 1804. The actual site of the meeting was across the Missouri River in Nebraska.

Western Historic Trails Center. http://www.iowahistory.org/sites/ western_trails/western_trails.html. Interpretive center for the Lewis and Clark Trail, Mormon Pioneer Trail, Oregon Trail, and California Trail, with Native American exhibits.

Davenport

Black Hawk Purchase Treaty Marker. In LeClaire Park at the bottom of Harrison Street near the Mississippi River. Treaty signed on site of present East 5th Street between Farnum and LeClaire streets in Davenport.

Putnam Museum of History and Natural Science. http://www.putnam .org. Exhibits on archaeology (including Woodland period pottery) and regional history with an emphasis on the Quad Cities area, copy of the Black Hawk Treaty, and records of the Davenport hoax.

Des Moines and Urbandale

Iowa Genealogical Society. http://www.iowagenealogy.org. Active since 1965, the society has an extensive library.

Living History Farms. http://www.livinghistoryfarms.org. Several living history exhibits, including the re-creation of an Ioway village with bark lodges, gardens, and artifacts.

State Historical Society of Iowa Museum. http://www.iowahistory
.org/museum/index.html. Located in the Des Moines branch of
the State Historical Society of Iowa along with the State Archives
of Iowa and an extensive library, the museum contains extensive
historical and archaeological displays on Iowa's Native Americans.

State Library of Iowa. http://www.statelibraryofiowa.org. Includes
the State Documents Center.

Dubuque

Heritage Trail. http://www.dubuquecounty.com/HeritageTrail.cfm.
Twenty-six miles of former railroad bed converted into a hiking
and biking trail that runs past Indian mounds and lead-mining
sites. Closed in 2008 due to flooding; check before visiting.

Little Maquoketa River Mounds Preserve. http://www.Dubuque
county.com/Nature.cfm. At least thirty-two Woodland mounds
on forty-one acres.

Mines of Spain Recreation Area. www.iowadnr.com/parks/state
_park_list/mines_spain.html. Dubuque is named for Julien
Dubuque, a French miner who arrived in 1788 and helped develop
the lead mines belonging to the Meskwaki, Sauk, and Ioway there.
His claim was recognized by Spain, which controlled Iowa at the
time. The land grant was named the Mines of Spain. A monument overlooks the Mississippi River from the south end of Julien
Dubuque Drive in the Mines of Spain area. Site of Native American
lead-mining efforts, primarily by the Meskwaki.

National Mississippi River Museum and Aquarium. http://www
.mississippirivermuseum.com. Covers three hundred years of river
history; includes exhibits on local Indian history.

Fort Atkinson

Fort Atkinson State Preserve. http://www.iowadnr.com/parks/state
_park_list/fort_atkinson.html. 1840s buildings, foundation, and
museum. Used to protect the Winnebago and keep peace between
the Sauk and Meskwaki and the Sioux. The Fort Atkinson Rendez-
vous is held the last full weekend in September.

Fort Dodge

Fort Dodge Historical Museum and Frontier Village. http://www
.fortmuseum.com. Replica of military fort and frontier town with
twelve historic and replica buildings. Museum with Indian, pioneer, and military artifacts.

Fort Madison

Old Fort Madison. http://www.oldfortmadison.com. Built in 1808
and used during the War of 1812, the original fort was destroyed
in 1813 by the Sauk and Meskwaki when it was abandoned by U.S.
forces; the present structure is a replica.

Glenwood

Mills County Historical Museum. http://www.millscountymuseum
.org. Displays of fifteen thousand Indian artifacts and exhibits on
the nearby Glenwood site, including a reconstruction of a prehistoric earthlodge.

Guttenberg

Turkey River Mounds. From Guttenberg drive 4.5 miles southeast
on U.S. 52. The site is reached by a very steep trail up to a two
hundred-foot-high ridge above the Turkey and Mississippi rivers,
where forty-five conical and linear Woodland mounds can be seen.

Harper's Ferry

Effigy Mounds National Monument. http://www.nps.gov/efmo. Over two hundred Woodland period effigy mounds (most in the shape of bears or birds), conical, and linear mounds. Visitor center and museum with artifact exhibits and audiovisual presentation, interpretive trails through mound areas.

Homestead

Indian Fishtraps, Amana Nature Trail. http://www.cs.uiowa.edu/~ jones/natural/amana.html. During low water, especially in late summer, the remains of a stone structure used by Indians to catch fish can be seen.

Iowa City

Office of the State Archaeologist and Iowa Archeological Society. http://www.uiowa.edu/~osa. http://www.uiowa.edu/~osa/IAS/index .html. Located at 700 S. Clinton Street south of the University of Iowa campus.

State Historical Society of Iowa. http://www.iowahistory.org/ library/library_offers/microfilm_loan_purchase.html. Largest collection of Iowa historical documents.

University of Iowa. http://www.uiowa.edu. The Museum of Natural History has excellent exhibits and dioramas on the natural history of Iowa as well as Indian history and archaeology (PaleoIndian, Archaic, Woodland, Great Oasis, Mill Creek, Glenwood, and Oneota), with special attention to the historic Meskwaki, Ioway, and Sauk. The university also hosts a popular powwow in the spring.

Keokuk

Grave and Statue of Keokuk. Between 15th and 17th Streets, at the north end of Rand Park, overlooking the Mississippi River.

Keosauqua

Lacey-Keosauqua State Park. http://www.iowadnr.gov/parks/state
_park_list/lacey_keo.html. In the northwest part of the park are
nineteen Woodland mounds.

Kingston

Malchow Mounds. A group of fifty-eight mounds from the Woodland period. Near the Kingston Oneota site.

Le Claire

Buffalo Bill Museum. http://www.buffalobillmuseumleclaire.com.
Collections include Indian artifacts.

Lehigh

Dolliver Memorial State Park. http:www.iowadnr.com/parks/state
_park_list/dolliver.html. The park's attractions include three
Woodland mounds and a ravine that may have served as a buffalo
jump, a site where buffalo were stampeded over a cliff by Indian
hunters. Damaged by flooding in 2008; check before visiting.

Marshalltown

Historical Society of Marshall County. http://www.marshallhistory
.org. Collections include Indian artifacts.

McGregor

Pikes Peak State Park. http://www.iowadnr.com/parks/state_park
_list/pikes_peak.html. Several mounds on a bluff above the Mississippi River, including a bear effigy mound.

Meskwaki Settlement near Tama

Meskwaki Annual Powwow. http://www.meskwaki.org/special/powwow/mapa.html. Takes place in August. Arts and crafts, food vendors, and traditional dancing.

Meskwaki Casino. http://www.meskwaki.com. The Meskwaki tribal casino, which has provided an economic turnaround for the tribe, funds tribal programs and annuities.

Missouri Valley

Harrison County Historical Village. http://www.harrisoncounty parks.org/welcome. Large collection of Indian artifacts.

Mount Vernon

Palisades-Kepler State Park. http://www.iowadnr.com/parks/state _park_list/palisades.html. Numerous Indian mounds from the Woodland period.

New Albin

Fish Farm Mounds. About thirty mounds from the Woodland period, with trail.

Ocheyedan

Ocheyedan Mound. http://www.osceolacountyia.com/ocheyedan/ochMound.htm. A natural feature rather than an Indian mound, this is a sacred site.

Okoboji Lake and Spirit Lake

Several cabin sites associated with the Spirit Lake Massacre have markers, most accessed from Highway 71, including the Granger Cabin (Okoboji Town Hall lawn), the Howe Cabin (north of the

YWCA), the original Gardner Cabin and the Luce Cabin (both on Pillsbury Point, West Okoboji Lake), the Mattock Cabin (north edge of Arnolds Park), and the Noble Cabin (1 mile north of the Howe Cabin). The Spirit Lake stockade, on the front lawn of the courthouse, was built to protect settlers in the wake of the Spirit Lake Massacre.

Onawa

Casino Omaha. http://www.casinocity.com/us/ia/onawa/omaha. Casino of the Omaha Tribe of Nebraska.

Oskaloosa

Statue of Mahaska. Located in the park at the courthouse, this sculptural representation of Ioway Chief Mahaska I, made by Sherry Edmundson Fry, won the Rome Prize in 1908.

Ottumwa

Wapello County Historical Museum. Exhibits on local prehistory and history, with Indian artifacts.

Prairie City

Prairie Learning Center, Neal Smith National Wildlife Refuge. http://www.tallgrass.org. Site of the largest prairie reconstruction in the world, containing a herd of grazing buffalo, it also has excellent interactive exhibits that focus on the natural and cultural history of the local prairies.

Rock Rapids

Blood Run National Historic Landmark. http://www.iowahistory .org/sites/blood_run/blood_run.html. Probably the largest Oneota village and burial site in the United States. Tribes connected with this site include Omaha, Ponca, Ioway, Otoe, Arikara, and Yankton Sioux. The site is on both sides of the Big Sioux River in Iowa and South Dakota. There were once two hundred mounds, half of which remain. Other remains include boulder circles and pitted boulders.

Sidney

Fremont County Historical Museum Complex. http://www.sidneyia.net/museum/php. Multibuilding complex and American Indian room with artifacts.

Sioux City

Sioux City Public Museum. http://www.siouxcitymuseum.org. Collections include northwest Iowa artifacts and ethnological exhibits from the region.

War Eagle Monument. Near W. 4th and Burton Streets, grave of Yankton chief War Eagle, with memorial.

Sloan

WinnaVegas. http://www.winnavegas.biz. Casino of the Winnebago Tribe of Nebraska.

Sutherland

Wittrock Indian Village National Historic Landmark. East of Sutherland; access permission required from private landowner. Mill Creek village with homes and defensive earthworks.

Swisher

Curtis Hill Indian Museum. Largest private museum of Native American artifacts in Iowa. Thousands of projectile points, collections of points from other states, collection of southwest and Mississippian pottery, hundreds of pipes, grooved axes, bone tools, and beadwork.

Toledo

Tama County Historical Museum. http://www.tamatoledo.com/ attractions.html. Collections include Meskwaki clothing and tools.

Toolesboro

Toolesboro Mounds National Historic Landmark and State Preserve. http://www.iowahistory.org/historic-sites/toolesboro-mounds. Five acres of Hopewell Woodland mounds, a demonstration prairie plot, and a visitor center with new exhibits on the Woodland and Oneota cultures.

Wapello

Louisa County Historical Society Museum. Prehistoric and historic American Indian artifacts.

Waterloo

Grout Museum of History and Science. http://www.groutmuseum district.org. Exhibits cover PaleoIndians, Archaic, the start of Indian farming, and historic Indians of Iowa.

Waukon

Old Courthouse Museum. http://www.allamakeehistory.org/index .html.

Slinde Mounds State Preserve. About fifteen Woodland mounds overlooking the Upper Iowa River; visiting involves a fairly strenuous half-mile hike.

TRIBAL CONTACTS

Only official tribal websites, when available, are given here; other websites with information on tribes can be found in the next section, Recommended Books and Websites. Addresses are accurate as of May 2009.

Illinois Confederacy

Peoria Tribe of Indians of Oklahoma
118 S. Eight Tribes Trail
P.O. Box 1527
Miami OK 74355
http://www.peoriatribe.com

Ioway

Iowa Tribe of Kansas and Nebraska
Route 1, Box 58-A
White Cloud KS 66094

Iowa Tribe of Oklahoma
R.R. 1, Box 721
Perkins OK 74059
http://www.iowanation.org

Meskwaki

Sac and Fox of the Mississippi in Iowa
349 Meskwaki Road
Tama IA 52339
http://www.meskwaki.org

Omaha and Ponca

Omaha Tribe of Nebraska
100 Main Street
P.O. Box 368
Macy NE 68039

Ponca Tribe of Nebraska
P.O. Box 288
Niobrara NE 68760

Otoe and Missouria

Otoe-Missouria Tribe
P.O. Box 68
Red Rock OK 74056

Pawnee and Arikara

Pawnee Tribe
P.O. Box 470
Pawnee OK 74058
http://www.pawneenation.org

Three Affiliated Tribes (Arikara, Mandan, Hidatsa)
404 Frontage Road
New Town ND 58763
http://www.mhanation.com

Potawatomi

Prairie Band Potawatomi
16281 Q Road
Mayetta KS 66509
http://www.pbpindiantribe.com

Santee and Yankton Sioux

Prairie Island Indian Community (Mdewakanton)
5636 Sturgeon Lake Road
Welch MN 55089
http://www.prairieisland.org

Santee Sioux Tribe of Nebraska
425 Frazier Avenue N., Suite 2
Niobrara NE 68760
http://www.santeedakota.org

Yankton Sioux Tribe
P.O. Box 248
Marty SD 57361

Sauk

Sac and Fox Nation
Route 2, Box 246
Stroud OK 74079
http://www.cowboy.net/native/sacnfox.html

Sac and Fox Nation of Missouri
Route 1, Box 60
Reserve KS 66434
http://www.sacandfoxcasino.com

Winnebago-Hochunk

Ho-Chunk Nation
W9814 Airport Road
Black River Falls WI 54615
http://www.hochunknation.com

Winnebago Tribe of Nebraska
P.O. Box 687
Winnebago NE 68071
http://www.winnebagotribe.com

RECOMMENDED BOOKS AND WEBSITES

Books for Younger Readers

Anderson, Bernice. *Indian Sleep-Man Tales.* New York: Bramhall House, 1970.

Anderson, Madelyn Klein. *The Omaha.* New York: Franklin Watts, 2000.

Bonvillain, Nancy. *The Santee Sioux.* New York: Chelsea House, 1996.

Eastman, Charles A. *Indian Boyhood.* New York: Dover Publications, 1971.

Ferris, Jeri. *Native American Doctor: The Story of Susan La Flesche Picotte.* Minneapolis: Carolrhoda Books, 1991.

Hoover, Herbert T. *The Yankton Sioux.* New York: Chelsea House, 1988.

Irwin, Hadley. *We Are Mesquakie; We Are One.* Old Westbury, N.Y.: Feminist Press, 1980.

Lacey, Theresa Jensen, and Frank Porter. *The Pawnee.* New York: Chelsea House, 1996.

McDaniel, Melissa. *The Sac and Fox.* New York: Chelsea House, 1995.

Porter, Frank, and James A. Clifton. *Potawatomi.* New York: Chelsea House, 1987.

Powell, Suzanne. *The Potawatomi.* New York: Franklin Watts, 1998.

Von Ahnen, Katherine. *Charlie Young Bear.* Niwot, Colo.: Roberts Rinehart, 1994.

Walters, Anna Lee. *The Pawnee Nation.* Mankato, Minn.: Bridgestone Books, 2000.

———, and Carole Bowles. *The Two-Legged Creature: An Otoe Story.* Flagstaff, Ariz.: Northland, 1993.

Zitkala-Sa. *American Indian Stories.* Lincoln: University of Nebraska Press, 1986.

Books for Older Readers

Illinois Confederacy

Matson, Nehemiah, and Rodney O. Davis. *French and Indians of the Illinois River.* Carbondale: Southern Illinois University Press, 2001.

Ioway

Blaine, Martha Royce. *The Ioway Indians.* Norman: University of Oklahoma Press, 1995.

Foster, Lance M. *Sacred Bundles of the Ioway Indians.* Santa Fe, N.M.: Native Nations Press, 2004.

Peltier, Jerome, and Edward Kowrach. *Madame Dorion.* Fairfield, Wash.: Ye Galleon Press, 1980.

Meskwaki

Edmunds, R. David, and Joseph Peyser. *The Fox Wars: The Mesquakie Challenge to New France.* Norman: University of Oklahoma Press, 1993.

McTaggart, Fred. *Wolf That I Am: In Search of the Red Earth People.* Norman: University of Oklahoma Press, 1994.

Torrence, Gaylord, and Robert Hobbs. *Art of the Red Earth People.* Seattle: University of Washington Press, 1989.

Young Bear, Ray A. *Black Eagle Child: The Facepaint Narratives.* Iowa City: University of Iowa Press, 1992.

———. *Remnants of the First Earth.* New York: Grove Press, 1996.

———. *The Rock Island Hiking Club.* Iowa City: University of Iowa Press, 2001.

Zielinski, John. *Mesquakie and Proud of It.* Kalona, Iowa: Photo-Art Gallery, 1976.

Omaha and Ponca

Fletcher, Alice, and Francis La Flesche. *The Omaha Tribe.* Lincoln: University of Nebraska Press, 1972.

Howard, James. *The Ponca Tribe.* Lincoln: University of Nebraska Press, 1995.

La Flesche, Francis. *Ke-Ma-Ha: The Omaha Stories of Francis La Flesche.* Lincoln: University of Nebraska Press, 1998.

Ridington, Robin, and Dennis Hastings. *Blessing for a Long Time: The Sacred Pole of the Omaha Tribe.* Lincoln: University of Nebraska Press, 1997.

Tibbles, Thomas Henry, and Kay Graber. *Standing Bear and the Ponca Chiefs.* Lincoln: University of Nebraska Press, 1995.

Tong, Benson. *Susan La Flesche Picotte, M.D.: Omaha Indian Leader and Reformer.* Norman: University of Oklahoma Press, 1999.

Otoe and Missouria

Chapman, Berlin Basil. *The Otoes and Missourias.* Oklahoma City: Times Journal Publishing Co., 1965.

Walters, Anna Lee. *Talking Indian: Reflections on Survival and Writing.* Ithaca, N.Y.: Firebrand Books, 1992.

Pawnee and Arikara

Grinnell, George Bird. *Pawnee Hero Stories and Folk-Tales.* Lincoln: University of Nebraska Press, 1990.

Hyde, George. *The Pawnee Indians.* Norman: University of Oklahoma Press, 1988.

Weltfish, Gene. *The Lost Universe: Pawnee Life and Culture.* Lincoln: University of Nebraska Press, 1990.

Potawatomi

Clifton, James A. *The Prairie People: Continuity and Change in Potawatomi Indian Culture, 1665–1965.* Iowa City: University of Iowa Press, 1998.

Santee and Yankton Sioux

Anderson, Gary C. *Kinsmen of Another Kind: Dakota-White Relations in the Upper Mississippi Valley, 1650–1862.* Lincoln: University of Nebraska Press, 1984.

———. *Little Crow: Spokesman for the Sioux.* St. Paul: Minnesota Historical Society Press, 1986.

Deloria, Vine, Jr. *Singing for a Spirit.* Santa Fe: Clear Light, 1999.

Rappaport, Doreen, and Zitkala-Sa. *The Flight of Red Bird: The Life of Zitkala-Sa.* New York: Puffin, 1999.

Spector, Janet D. *What This Awl Means: Feminist Archaeology at a Wahpeton Dakota Village.* St. Paul: Minnesota Historical Society Press, 1993.

Sauk

Hagan, William. *The Sac and Fox Indians.* Norman: University of Oklahoma Press, 1988.

Jackson, Donald, ed. *Black Hawk: An Autobiography.* Urbana: University of Illinois Press, 1990.

Trask, Kerry A. *Black Hawk: The Battle for the Heart of America.* New York: Henry Holt, 2006.

Winnebago-Hochunk

Fikes, Jay C. *Reuben Snake, Your Humble Serpent.* Santa Fe: Clear Light Publishers, 1996.

Lurie, Nancy. *Mountain Wolf Woman.* Ann Arbor: University of Michigan Press, 1974.

Radin, Paul. *The Road of Life and Death.* Princeton: Princeton University Press, 1991.

———. *The Winnebago.* Lincoln: University of Nebraska Press, 1990.

Smith, David Lee. *Folklore of the Winnebago.* Norman: University of Oklahoma Press, 1997.

General

Ballantine, Betty, and Ian Ballantine, eds. *The Native Americans: An Illustrated History.* Atlanta: Turner Publishing, 1993.

Bataille, Gretchen M., David Mayer Gradwohl, and Charles Silet. *The Worlds between Two Rivers: Perspectives on American Indians in Iowa.* Iowa City: University of Iowa Press, 2000.

————, and Laurie Lisa. *Native American Women: A Biographical Dictionary.* New York: Routledge, 2001.

Davis, Mary, ed. *Native America in the Twentieth Century: An Encyclopedia.* New York: Garland Press, 1996.

Deloria, Vine, Jr. *Custer Died for Your Sins.* Norman: University of Oklahoma Press, 2003.

DeMallie, Raymond, and William C. Sturtevant, eds. *Handbook of North American Indians.* Vol. 13: *Plains.* Washington, D.C.: Smithsonian Institution, 2001.

Faldet, David S. *Oneota Flow: The Upper Iowa River and Its People.* Iowa City: University of Iowa Press, 2009.

O'Brien, Sharon. *American Indian Tribal Governments.* Norman: University of Oklahoma Press, 1989.

Sturtevant, William C., ed. *Handbook of North American Indians.* Vol. 15: *Northeast.* Washington, D.C.: Smithsonian Institution, 1978.

Thorne, Tanis C. *The Many Hands of My Relations: French and Indians on the Lower Missouri.* Columbia: University of Missouri Press, 1996.

Tiller, Veronica, ed. *Tiller's Guide to Indian Country: Economic Profiles of American Indian Reservations.* Albuquerque: Bow Arrow Publishing, 1996.

Waldman, Carl, ed. *Encyclopedia of Native American Tribes.* New York: Checkmark Books, 1998.

Wright, Muriel H. *A Guide to the Indian Tribes of Oklahoma.* Norman: University of Oklahoma Press, 1987.

Archaeology
Alex, Lynn Marie. *Iowa's Archaeological Past.* Iowa City: University of Iowa Press, 2000.

Anderson, Duane. *Eastern Iowa Prehistory.* Ames: Iowa State University Press, 1981.

————. *Western Iowa Prehistory.* Ames: Iowa State University Press, 1975.

Boszhardt, Robert F. *A Projectile Point Guide for the Upper Mississippi River Valley.* Iowa City: University of Iowa Press, 2003.

Morrow, Toby. *Iowa Projectile Points.* Iowa City: Office of the State Archaeologist, University of Iowa, 1984.

Theler, James L., and Robert F. Boszhardt. *Twelve Millennia: Archaeology of the Upper Mississippi River Valley.* Iowa City: University of Iowa Press, 2003.

Thomas, David Hurst. *Skull Wars: Kennewick Man, Archaeology, and the Battle for Native American Identity.* New York: Basic Books, 2002.

Tiffany, Joseph A., and Christian A. Driver. *A Guide to Projectile Points of Iowa.* Parts 1 and 2. Iowa City: University of Iowa Press, 2009.

History
Bakeman, Mary Hawker. *Legends, Letters, and Lies: Readings about Inkpaduta and the Spirit Lake Massacre of 1857.* Roseville, Minn.: Park Genealogical Books, 2001.

Horan, James. *The McKenney-Hall Portrait Gallery of American Indians.* New York: Crown, 1972.

Tanner, Helen Hornbeck, ed. *The Atlas of Great Lakes Indian History.* Norman: University of Oklahoma Press, 1987.

Whittaker, William E., ed. *Frontier Forts of Iowa: Indians, Traders, and Soldiers, 1682–1862.* Iowa City: University of Iowa Press, 2009.

Places and Landscapes
Burke, William J. *The Upper Mississippi Valley: How the Landscape Shaped Our Heritage.* Waukon: Mississippi Valley Press, 2000.

Kennedy, Frances H. *American Indian Places: A Historical Guidebook.* Lincoln: University of Nebraska Press, 2008.

Sayre, Robert F., ed. *Recovering the Prairie.* Madison: University of Wisconsin Press, 1996.

Stone, Larry A., and Iowa Department of Natural Resources. *Iowa: Portrait of the Land*. Des Moines: Iowa Department of Natural Resources, 2000.

Vogel, Virgil F. *Iowa Place Names of Indian Origin*. Iowa City: University of Iowa Press, 1983.

Religion and Spiritual Ways

Arbogast, Doyle. *Wounded Warriors: A Time for Healing*. Omaha: Little Turtle Publications, 1995.

Beck, Peggy, Anna Walters, and Lee Walters. *Sacred Ways of Knowledge: Sources of Life*. Tsaile, Ariz.: Navajo Community College Press, 2000.

Deloria, Vine, Jr. *God Is Red: A Native View of Religion*. Golden, Colo.: North American Press, 2003.

Websites

Web addresses are accurate as of May 2009.

American Indian Genealogy Forum
http://genforum.genealogy.com/ai

American Local History Network: Iowa
http://freepages.history.rootsweb.com/~rkross/ia-alhn

Black Hawk and the Black Hawk War of 1832
http://lincoln.lib.niu.edu/blackhawk

Contemporary Issues about Native American Art
http://www.nativetech.org/art/issues.html

The Encyclopedia of Hotcâk (Winnebago) Mythology
http://hotcakencyclopedia.com

The Illini Confederacy: Lords of the Mississippi Valley
http://members.tripod.com/~RFester/index.html

Indian Arts and Crafts
http://www.doi.gov/iacb/consumer-tips.html

Indian Country: Ho-Chunk
http://www.mpm.edu/wirp/ICW-223.html

Indianz.com.
http://www.indianz.com

Iowa GenWeb Project
http://iagenweb.org

Ioway Cultural Institute
http://ioway.nativeweb.org/home.htm

Meskwaki Anthology
http://www.meskwaki.bia.edu/history/MeskinteractiveCD1/
Pages/QuotesObservations/ObservationsIntro.htm

Moh He Hump Gah
http://firstpeople.iwarp.com

Native American Indian Genealogy Webring
http://members.tripod.com/~kjunkutie/natvrng.htm

Native American Sites
http://www.nativeculturelinks.com/indians.html

Native Tech
http://www.nativetech.org

Omaha Indian Music
http://memory.loc.gov/ammem/omhhtml

Omaha-Ponca Language
http://spot.colorado.edu/~koontz/omaha/op_sketch.htm

Pawnee Language Program
http://www.indiana.edu/~aisri/projects/pawnee

Red Men of Iowa
http://yawp.com/redmen

Sauk and Fox History
http://www.tolatsga.org/sf.html

State Historical Society of Iowa's Family History Research Tips
http://www.iowahistory.org/library/family_history/research
_tips.html

Winnebago History
http://www.dickshovel.com/win.html

INDEX

Other University of Iowa Press Books of Interest

The Biographical Dictionary of Iowa
Edited by David Hudson, Marvin Bergman, and Loren Horton

Buxton: A Black Utopia in the Heartland
By Dorothy Schwieder, Joseph Hraba, and Elmer Schwieder

A Country So Full of Game: The Story of Wildlife in Iowa
By James J. Dinsmore

The Emerald Horizon: The History of Nature in Iowa
By Cornelia F. Mutel

Frontier Forts of Iowa: Indians, Traders, and Soldiers, 1682–1862
Edited by William E. Whittaker

A Guide to Projectile Points of Iowa, Part 1: Paleoindian, Late Paleoindian, Early Archaic, and Middle Archaic Points, Part 2: Middle Archaic, Late

Archaic, Woodland, and Late Prehistoric Points
By Joseph A. Tiffany

Iowa: The Middle Land
By Dorothy Schwieder

An Iowa Album: A Photographic History, 1860–1920
By Mary Bennett

Iowa Past to Present: The People and the Prairie
By Dorothy Schwieder, Thomas Morain, and Lynn Nielsen

Iowa Stereographs: Three-Dimensional Visions of the Past
By Mary Bennett and Paul C. Juhl

Iowa's Archaeological Past
By Lynn M. Alex

Little Bit Know Something: Stories in a Language of Anthropology
By Robin Ridington